What Michael's Clients Say

"As **we tripled the size of our company over the past two and a half years,** Michael provided insight and recommendations for leadership, hiring, team building, negotiations and most importantly, goals and forecasts for the future."
— *Jolene McDonough, Owner/COO, Prudential California Realty*

"**We were able to decrease production costs by 40% while increasing gross revenue by 23%...** I believe that the company, my staff and I personally have benefited from the growth of my skills and increased confidence in handling the inevitable challenges associated with managing a small, growing business."
— *Deborah Mitchell, B.Sc.(Kin), C.Ped.(C), General Manager, Kintec Orthotics*

"I was in need of tools to move this company forward and into the next stage of growth effectively... **Thank you for making it fun to be in business again.**"
— *Dona Williamson, President, Precision Pumping Systems, Inc.*

"**I work fewer hours and make more money.** I'm more efficient and productive. I'm more focused in what I do day to day. Michael strongly suggested taking one week per month off — I laughed. Now I've been doing that for two years."
— *Allan Newbury, Financial Planner, CIBC Wood Gundy*

"**Michael helped us clarify our vision.** We were trying to do more things, and address more and more needs, but remain the same size. We were barely managing with the workload that we already had. We just wanted to serve people well, and respond to crises. Now we're positioned to do that."
— *Ernie Baatz, Spectrum Society for Community Living*

BUSINESS GROWTH by Design

A Business Owner's Guide to Tapping Your Potential Without Getting Tapped Out

Michael G. Walsh

KAIZEN CONSULTING SERVICES INC.
Vancouver · Denver · Reno · Chicago

Copyright © 2010 Kaizen Consulting Services Inc.

All rights reserved. No part of this book may be reproduced, stored in a retrieval system, or transmitted in any form or by any means, electronic, mechanical, photocopying, recording or otherwise, without the written permission of the author.

Disclaimer: This book is designed to provide information about the subject matter covered. It is sold with the understanding that the author is not engaged in rendering legal or accounting services. If legal or other expert assistance is required, the services of the appropriate professional should be sought.

It is the purpose of this book to provide you with possible strategies, though it is not necessarily your ultimate source of information as it may contain mistakes that are both typographical and in the content. The author shall have neither liability nor responsibility to any person or entity with respect to any loss or damage caused, or alleged to be caused, directly or indirectly by the information contained in this book.

If you do not wish to be bound by the above, you may return this publication to the seller for a full refund within three business days of purchase.

The tradenames "The 21st Century Entrepreneur", "The Business Builder" and "The Business Growth System" and their associated logos and trade dress are all trademarks belonging to Kaizen Consulting Services Inc. All other marks listed are the property of their respective owners.

Publisher: Kaizen Consulting Services Inc.
Design: Rivera Design Group Ltd.

601 West Broadway, Suite 400
Vancouver, BC Canada V5Z 4C2
Tel: 604-263-5670
Fax: 604-263-5641

www.kaizenconsulting.com   info@kaizenconsulting.com

In memory of my dad, Dr. Michael J. Walsh

Contents

FOREWORD   11

CHAPTER 1: INTRODUCTION   15
Introduction
Intended Outcomes
Making It Easier: The Notion of "Kaizen"
Building a Building vs. Building a Business
Criteria for Achieving Large-Scale Growth
Structuring for Growth: Overview

CHAPTER 2: CRITERIA   31
Criteria for Large-Scale Growth
    1. The Value Check
    2. The Market Check
    3. The Resource Check
    4. Respect for People
    5. Contributing to Others
    6. Contributing to Yourself
    7. The Power of People
    8. Gaining Input and Challenging the Norm
    9. The Growth Check
    10. The Strategic Check

CHAPTER 3: TAKE TIME OFF   57
The Three Zones
The Hidden Dynamic with Fatigue
My Personal Story
Steps for Taking Time Off
Exercise: Time Off
Risk-Managing Capacity

Chapter 4: Free Yourself Up   75
The Importance of This Step
First Things First
Delegation vs. Abdication
Activity Inventory and Ranking Templates

Chapter 5: Set Your Target   89
What Do You Want?
The Anatomy of Effective Goals
Exercise: Setting Some Initial Goals
Exercise: What Do You REALLY Want?
Financial Independence Calculator
Financial Significance Calculator

Chapter 6: Your Profit   109
What to Collect
The Income Statements
The Balance Sheet
The Customer List
Exercise: Your Profit
Exercise: Customer Profitability
Collecting Information: Follow-Up

Chapter 7: Customer Value   131
Your Value Proposition
The Credo
Exercise: What is Your Credo?
Your Process for Generating Customer Results
Evaluation of Solutions/Options Development
Example One: The Clarity Process™
Example Two: The Counterpoint Process
Your Unique Process

Exercise: What's Your Process?
The Customer Experience
Developing Your Marketing Materials

CHAPTER 8: ORGANIZATIONAL STRUCTURE   163
Thinking Through the Bigger Game
Your Organization Chart
Example: $10M Organization Chart
Outline for a Complete Business Plan Report
The Financial Statements
The Balance Sheet: Elements to Consider
Scaling Down the Model
Example: $5M Organization Chart
Building the Transition Plan
Example: $2M Organization Chart

CHAPTER 9: CASH FLOW   185
Measuring: The Income Statement
Backward Pricing
Steps
Purpose of the Cash Flow Forecast
Microsoft Office Excel
Example: Cash Flow Forecast

CHAPTER 10: PULLING IT ALL TOGETHER   203
Intended Outcomes Revisited
45-Point Checklist: Strategies for Large-Scale Growth

FOREWORD

I first met Michael Walsh on what can best be described as a blind date. Organizers of a conference had selected us to be teamed together for a presentation dealing with negotiation techniques. Michael's role was to focus on business lessons and mine was to supplement his commentary with real-life examples. Having never met each other before, it took me less than our first five minutes together to appreciate I was working with a person unlike anyone I had ever known. I also had no idea of the role Michael would have in the future transformation of my current business.

At the end of this event, I shared with him that our company was attempting to develop a succession strategy. With three partners and a staff of thirty people, we could see that within ten years we would need to have a plan to keep the business alive without the business founders. The company was full of great people, many of whom devoted their entire career to our organization. To someday announce that the business was closing, thank them for contributions and say "good luck" was not an option.

The partners and I then asked Michael, "How do we best become smaller?" He replied, "By getting bigger." At first, we didn't get it. In fact, the partnership at times rebelled against some of the propositions Michael put forward. But we persevered. As this book will share with you, implementing a large-scale growth business plan is not easy, and not for everybody, but I can relay it is absolutely possible.

I learned that some of the biggest obstacles to achieving large-scale growth are created by hanging on to old patterns of doing things supported by the state of your own attitude. You can choose to believe that the future can bring a radical transformation, or not. Without embracing the concept that circumstances can be altered for the better, however, you will not achieve success.

My first test came when I heard Michael state that we could triple our gross revenue within three years. Not only was this achievable, Michael assured us, it would be sustainable. This was, frankly, an outrageous statement as far as our partnership was concerned. The prospect of our business growing by even 50% over this time period seemed unrealistic to us. We, however, went about doing many of the things described in this book. Three years later our gross annual revenue had risen from $3.2 million to $10 million. We had exceeded Michael's projection.

When the recession hit our marketplace, and our competition was dealing with massive layoffs, we were still hiring. We went from three partners to nine in this period with a succession plan firmly in place. And although I now owned less of the company due to the expansion of the partnership, my personal annual income had tripled from what it was when we initiated our growth efforts.

There were also residual benefits to growing our business. The decision to take on a new challenge at relatively late stages in our careers has turned out to be a highly energizing endeavour. We now have a business that attracts talent due to our ability to provide a working environment that helps people accelerate their career goals. We evolved from being a business entity operated by individual partner silos to a powerful cohesive organization.

Partners are now watched carefully to ensure they each take six weeks of vacation per year. I came to appreciate that forging a great corporate future is all about achieving results, not about how many hours you put in. To plan time for rest and reflection, and to stick to that plan, is a prerequisite for a strategic leader. Otherwise, be prepared to feel burdened and stuck with old routines that are dependent upon your individual efforts. Separate being busy from being effective. In a leadership position, you still need to spend a lot of time on business matters, but if you can leverage your efforts rather than doing what you previously have done, it's time well spent.

Reading this book brought back many memories for me of past business coaching sessions with Michael. I can share that you might feel tested at times going through the various exercises presented here, because the end result might not be clear at first. This is where the belief factor comes into play: it defines what entrepreneurs are made of. Implementing large-scale growth requires diligence and the courage to help lead people to a brighter future. I've experienced it, but needed the kind of help provided here. Enjoy what Michael shares.

—Richard Bolus, Founding Partner,
CEI Architecture & Planning Interiors

CHAPTER I

Introduction

Introduction

Dear Business Owner,

Congratulations on taking this next step in the evolution of your business!

Whether you are a business owner with twenty-plus years of experience or a new entrepreneur, this is a very exciting time! For those of you who are willing to take action and follow the steps presented in this strategic guide, large-scale growth is within your reach. This system communicates the strategies I have used across a wide range of businesses—from startup companies to established companies with over $100 million in revenue. What I've learned from working with the more established companies benefits those of you who are just starting out, or who plan to grow to a much larger size.

There is a great deal to cover here. Many elements will compete for your attention as you seek to double, triple or quadruple your business within a relatively short period (one to four years). Unless you have already owned a business that has been at the size you want your current business to grow to, this will be new territory for you. You are choosing a path that few dare to follow, and the journey can be quite exhilarating (and at times precarious). By choosing this path you will discover that it can also be a rewarding learning experience. So, do you want to grow your business?

You may be asking yourself, what is the purpose of this strategic guide?

There is no more dangerous time in the evolution of a business than when it is in a period of growth. There is always a risk/reward relationship that comes with growth. When working toward large-scale growth, the game is accelerated — compressing and magnifying the many risks involved. The objective is accelerating the rewards associated with a larger organization, though you will find that the threats are often accelerated as well.

This book on growth strategies has been developed to aid you in thinking through the structure of large-scale growth, allowing you to manage your risks more effectively and making it easier to achieve the rewards you seek. The book will walk you through each of the major structural areas I have identified as critical in generating and sustaining profitable growth within your company, and how to remain consistent with your goals and commitments. My experience in achieving this with many companies over the past decade-plus gives me comfort in outlining these elements to you. I hope that this provides you with the clarity you will need to achieve your goals, regardless of their size.

Sincerely,

Michael Walsh
President,
Kaizen Consulting Services Inc.

Special Note

This book will take you through a number of steps in different areas of your business, and provide suggestions for what you may want to consider as you plan the growth of your company. My goal is to assist you with strategies, tactics and perspectives I used to support many other organizations to achieve large-scale growth.

Remember that each business is unique and, because of this, you must not blindly accept what is presented to you by anyone. As with anything in life, at the end of the day, you will be the best judge of what works for you and your business, and what does not. Be open to trying new ideas, but always use your own discernment when adapting the information to fit your personal situation. When in doubt, hire the services of a professional advisor to assist you further. Each entrepreneur's situation is different, and the nuances of each circumstance may have a large impact on the viability of a particular strategy. An advisor or mentor who has been, or is an active business owner can help you work through the issues at hand and give you an outsider's perspective that will be indispensable to you as you grow.

If you have your own advisor or mentor, great. If you need one, you are only a google search away.

Intended Outcomes

I have specific outcomes in mind for you to gain from your use of this strategic guide, and I have several objectives for you to meet through your interaction with this material:

1. I will give you clear, practical advice on accessing your own personal power and creative energy to achieve large-scale growth in your business.
2. I will help you clarify how much growth to aspire to.
3. I will guide you in building a game plan for large-scale growth in your business.

These are pretty tall orders. There is a great deal to consider when you are working toward achieving large-scale growth. However, by working through the steps I provide, you will be better able to achieve the outcomes you seek — for yourself and for your business.

Making It Easier: Using the Notion of "Kaizen"

There are a great number of moving parts to any business. As a result, even the thought of attempting large-scale growth may seem daunting, or downright overwhelming. In order to make this task more manageable, one perspective I suggest you adopt is to incorporate the concept of "kaizen".

Kaizen is a Japanese word meaning incremental growth or continuous improvement through doing little things better. By breaking things down to their sub-components (and sub-sub-components, and so on), difficult tasks become possible to achieve.

Each of the major issues and concerns a business owner faces may be broken down into a series of smaller items which, once clarified, are much easier to address. Through active work on what appear to be the little things, entrepreneurs are amazed at the lasting results they achieve. These results usually go straight to the bottom-line profits of a firm.

What Stops Us?

In school, we were trained to get the "right" answer. As far back as grade one, if we got a perfect score on a test, we got a star. All through school, perfection was rewarded; poor marks were shunned.

We have been very well trained to seek perfection. Yet this opposes the concept of kaizen. The philosophy of kaizen is that small, incremental adjustments or the fine-tuning of an existing situation are more effective than the all-or-nothing approach that is usually in place when people seek perfection.

Simply stated, the philosophy of kaizen might be summarized as follows:

Bad is better than nothing.
Good is better than bad.
Perfect is the enemy of good.

Bad is better than nothing: Life rewards action, not perfection. Too often people don't start tasks because they are afraid they will not get it right the first time. Yet if we do not take action, then no learning will ever take place. It is often easier to make adjustments once you have started something than it is to get started in the first place.

Good is better than bad: I have received very little resistance to this idea. But "perfect is the enemy of good"? Weren't we taught to seek perfection in everything we do? After all, we worked hard for those stars, and occasionally we got them.

How could perfect be the enemy of good?

Two reasons: First, if it needs to be perfect to be satisfactory, you may never get started. Second, if you ever declare something to be perfect, that means that you can never improve it further.

How does this apply to business growth?

It is quite common to see business owners struggle to manage their many commitments while trying to grow their businesses, which is not surprising considering all that is involved with large-scale growth. There is too much to do! You may become overwhelmed by just reading through the Contents section of this book.

Where do you start?

Using the notion of kaizen, we will take things one step at a time in order to sort out what is needed and when. Then, instead of trying to finish everything at once, we will do just one thing in a row (this will be a short row). The notion of kaizen is consistent with the old saying, "By the inch, it's a cinch. By the yard, it's hard."

At the end of this book is a forty-five-point checklist of actions to take to set you on your way toward large-scale growth. Nobody said that this level of growth would occur over night. However, if you just choose three to five actions to start — pick actions that feel good to you — then you will build the confidence you need to take — you got it — the next three to five actions, and so on, as you grow.

Building a Building vs. Building a Business

Did you know that over 50% of small businesses fail within three years, and 85% fail in the first five years? Did you also know that of the 15% of businesses that make it past year five, less than 10%

make it past year ten? Kind of makes you wonder what you've gotten yourself into, doesn't it? Now, if only ten out of one-hundred small businesses last ten years or longer, that means that ninety out of one-hundred don't make it.

But think about this: how many buildings fail (i.e. fall down) in the first five years? What do you think the complete failure rate of buildings is in the first five years? Zero, or very close to zero. How about the first ten years? Almost zero again.

In fact, clients of mine who are architects and engineers in both Canada and the USA tell me that the failure rate of complete buildings is so small that governments and housing commissions only measure the failure rate of the parts of a building — the roof anchors, the precast wall leaks, the defective caulking, etc. While these are important failures, they are minor compared to the falling down of a whole building.

Why is it that people can construct a building that lasts years, yet they can't construct businesses that last for anything close to the same amount of time? What is the difference?

Is it money? Is it the people? Is it the foundation? Is it the structure?

How about planning? The level of rigor and planning for a building is much higher than it is for most small businesses.

If the difference between building a durable building and building a lasting business is in the level of planning, what is it about the planning of the construction of a building that's different from the planning done to build a business?

How about certainty? Are you certain that you made thorough business plans? How certain were you about your business plans?

The government mandates the level of planning required for the construction of buildings. They have had experts generate a building code that specifies the level of planning that has to be done during building construction. The government dictates that you have to do enough planning to keep the building standing for decades. In Europe, it is for centuries.

Now, the majority of buildings do stay up for a long time. Building to the standards of the building code generally yields safe, efficient and long-lasting buildings.

A Level of Certainty

Are they just more safety conscious in the construction industry? What would happen if a building were to collapse? People would get hurt or possibly die. Now let's compare that with what happens when a small business fails. A few people lose some money. Some are upset. But nobody dies over it, do they? There are no government inquiries or blow-by-blow expert examinations of what went wrong, nor is there a public accounting of who didn't do what, is there?

There is also a second component required when erecting a building that is too often lacking in the building of a business. That is the periodic inspections done to ensure the building actually gets built as planned. This is why a business advisor, whether it is a consultant or a business coach, is so critical in business. While the planning is very important, it is just as important to ensure its implementation goes according to plan.

In a business, planning implementation is very difficult to achieve, since there are forces at play that keep constantly changing. This is where a seasoned, outside pair of eyes comes in handy. Just like a city inspector, your business consultant or coach will notice things that you may miss. He or she is looking from a different perspective.

Remember, once a building has been completed, it pretty much stays the way it was built (earthquakes aside). After a period of "settling" over the first year or two, it doesn't normally move. However, for a business, the environment keeps changing, generating the ongoing need for constant planning and adjusting to keep up with, and stay ahead of, the changes in the market taking place.

What would happen if you planned your business and inspected its actions to the same level and precision as they do with buildings? What do you think might happen? Would you get predictable business growth? Yes. We've seen it happen consistently.

For those of you who currently work with consultants, coaches and other mentors, very smart! For those who don't, yet, maybe it's time to start. If you can't afford a business coach, get a mentor who has owned (or owns) a business as big as you would like yours to grow. Find someone in your geographic area who can help you navigate, using a set of eyes that is outside of your business. You may well find that this person becomes your biggest ally in the profitable growth of your company. Very few people who are super-successful financially got there based upon what they already knew. They learned either from their mistakes — which can be very expensive — or they learned from others. Find a mentor who can provide a rich, third-party perspective on your business. You would be surprised how many retired or semi-retired business owners would love to share their experiences to support you in your goals. Their wisdom is often hard-won and it is a true acknowledgement of their success to be able to pass along gems that might help.

What you may find is that much of the small business planning and structural advice in books is adapted from large business models or the needs of banks. While that meets the specific needs of large businesses and financial institutions, it's just not as useful for your small business.

Seek out advice that is appropriate to your current size of business and the size of your planned growth. A little time spent in researching an appropriate match of coach, consultant, retired business owner or mentor for your business will go a long way in supporting you to achieve your goals for growth.

What follows is a summary of what you will find in the rest of this book.

Criteria for Achieving Large-Scale Growth

When I work with clients who want their businesses to grow, I begin by looking at ten specific criteria. If you are not sure whether these criteria are present in your situation, please read through chapter 2 carefully. This will help you identify any of the areas that may need to be bolstered or improved in order for you to step into large-scale growth.

Structuring for Growth: Overview

There are a number of elements necessary to achieve large-scale growth. This book will provide you with the processes you need to develop the appropriate structures for your particular business. While different businesses need different structures, the focus here is on the process of sorting out yours, regardless of what business you are in.

This system will help you to do these eight things.

Take Time Off

One of the essential elements for growth is for you to have all your wits about you. In order to achieve that state, what do you think the effect of taking time for yourself will be, not just at the beginning of the process but on an ongoing basis? You will need to be fresh to think through—and then take on—the process of implementing large-scale growth. Let's examine the impact of this simple step in detail to show you how important it is to get the rest you need to achieve what you want.

Free Yourself Up

Anyone can talk about wanting to grow, but if you are already too busy maintaining your current business, then where do you find the time to grow it? How do you free yourself up so that you will have the time to grow your business in a way that is consistent with your goals?

Set Your Target

I have designed a series of questions to help you to clarify exactly what you want from your business. A business can be set up as a tool to serve and support the goals and commitments of its owners. Too often, however, a small business ends up enslaving its owners to its care. With proper structuring and some reasonable growth, this dilemma can be averted or reversed, so that the business may do what it was intended to do — to give you what you want. However, in order for it to do this, you first need to figure out what it is that you want.

Examine Your Profit

Now we get to the meat of the meal (or the tofu, for you vegetarians). This is the first of the two most important aspects of running and growing a business. In a business, there is your profit, and there is customer value. Together, they form a value exchange that is the basis of all businesses, big or small. Without the synergy of the value exchange, there is no business.

In examining your profit, the following issues will be addressed:
- Which financial information you need to gather and analyze
- How to assemble your information to make it easier to see the trends
- What to look for in your financial statements
- The impact of your customer lists on your future profitability
- How to figure out your strategy
- The first steps to take to increase your profits as you grow

Clarify Your Customer Value

This is the other half of the value proposition. Your profit will only be sustained if your customers continue to gain value from their interactions with you and keep spending money on your goods and services.

This segment will examine:
- How you clarify your value proposition for your most profitable customers
- How to clarify your unique factors
- What is your DESIRED customer experience of value
- What is the ACTUAL experience of value that your current customers gain, and how you can measure that using customer satisfaction surveys
- How to develop your Unique Process and how to label it
- How to develop or enhance your marketing materials to communicate the customer value in a manner that will attract more of the best customers for you

Develop Your Organizational Structure

One of the critical elements of large-scale growth is to think through how the company will work at its larger size. In order to do this, I will be working through a series of steps that will allow you to see the bigger picture and to sort out which steps you need to take in order to get there.

This will include:
- Clarifying your current organizational structure
- Identifying the organization chart for your future, bigger company
- Crystallizing the key roles that will need to be filled
- Developing the interim levels of staffing that you will need in the short term
- Dovetailing your current staff with the evolving structure of your company
- Dealing with any people who don't fit into your future plans

Clarify Your Cash Flow

A strategy for the growth of your company would not be complete if it didn't include a plan for your cash flow. Profit is important, but in a growing business, cash is king. Expansion costs money, and it will eat up your cash if you are not careful. There are many relevant issues to address and this book offers a number of strategies that will help you to address them. This segment of the planning process deals with the all-important issue of cash flow.

Pull It All Together

The structural components of a growing company need to be constantly evolving to allow your business to grow the way you want it to. After covering the components listed above, I will pull everything together into one coordinated, integrated system that you can review frequently while growing your company to new and higher levels. This system includes checklists, worksheets and a step-by-step formula on how to get these areas working together as you grow.

Use the checklist at the end of the book as you put your strategic development plan into action.

CHAPTER 2

Criteria

Criteria

In order to prepare for large-scale growth, please ensure that each of the following criteria have been met in your company. If any of these are missing, you would be well advised to work on them first, and only then move toward large-scale growth.

Here are the criteria.

Criteria for Large-Scale Growth

1. You have a product or service that already delivers measurable value to your customers in the marketplace.
2. The market is large enough to allow for desired levels of growth.
3. You have access to the resources needed to scale the company (e.g. talented people) on a cost-effective basis.
4. You have a fundamental desire to contribute significantly to the lives of others.
5. You also have a fundamental desire to contribute significantly to yourself.
6. You have a core level of respect for people.
7. You believe in the power of people to accomplish extraordinary things in life (the human spirit is a very interesting dynamic that can accomplish amazing things; that is what business people need to tap to grow big time).
8. You are open to outside input and are willing to try new things and to challenge conventional norms (nobody who achieved sustained financial success got there based solely upon what they already knew).

9. You are willing to do what it takes (including potentially uncomfortable shifts if appropriate) to grow both personally and professionally as the company grows.
10. You are committed to staying strategic and to trust yourself, including trusting your own ability to discern what makes sense to you (don't just blindly trust others).

If you don't have all of these elements present in your business, work through the following section to help you properly prepare so that you may improve the odds.

1. The Value Check

Do you offer a product or service that delivers measurable value in the marketplace?

Are you giving your customers and clients measurable value at your current size? If not, then the first thing to do is to shore up this area before considering further growth.

Many business owners languish at a particular size of business because they have already grown past their ability to get everything done. As a result, they feel like they have been spread too thin. They are committed to giving their customers exceptional service, but they are not doing as much as they would like — they just can't seem to get to everything, and the odd time, customer service seems to slide a bit. Too often, it's more than just the odd time. This spells danger to a company at any size, not just to your plans for growth.

Several years ago, I was approached by a small but well-established printing company whose owner expressed a strong desire to grow through increased sales. He and his family had been in business for over fifteen years, running the company on a couple of two-color presses. However, other companies with faster and less expensive technology started taking some of his market share. The owner bought a used four-color press to keep up.

This created a dilemma for him: He no longer had enough business to feed the presses and cover the increased costs. The harder the owner tried, the tougher things became. He was running back and forth between trying to increase his customer base in sales, and overseeing the new, larger production crew. So, he decided to hire more salespeople than the one who had already been helping him for years.

By the time I was introduced to the company, they had three salespeople — all new within the last year — and the results coming in were sporadic from all three. The original salesperson had left some time before, and the owner was having trouble getting the sales team to work consistently. The biggest issue (as it often is with salespeople) seemed to be the downward price pressures from customers. Unless they were the cheapest, they didn't seem to get the work. They used to have an excellent reputation with their customers, but over the years, loyalty began to slip and customers were moving to competitors who had more **competitive pricing**.

I started working with their sales staff on strategies to support them in changing the basis of comparison away from price and onto "fit to need," a strategy the company had formerly employed successfully for many years. I helped the salespeople clarify the company's **unique selling proposition** in the market. By helping them focus on their established networks and work more through word of mouth, the salespeople started to generate increased sales.

Then the real problem started showing up: it turned out that every time the company got busy, it would tax the old four-color printing machine, which never did work very well and was badly in need of repair. The owner didn't have the money to fix this machine properly, so he would conduct band-aid-level repairs to keep it limping along. His thought was that if he could only get a few big jobs, they would pay enough for him to be able to fix the machine and move forward in a substantial way.

However, this never happened. Instead, every time one of his salespeople got a big job, the production crew would inevitably have a problem with breakdowns on the big printer. After doing the job wrong on that machine, they would have to redo it using multiple runs on the two-color machines they had. Each job lost them a little more money.

After digging further, through customer satisfaction surveys, I found that deteriorating quality was the single biggest reason that their loyal customers were abandoning ship. The redos were hurting not only their ability to keep customer promises, but hurting their profitability as well. The turnover in sales staff was the result of frustration at making promises to customers that the production crew could not keep — promises that competitors with better equipment were easily meeting.

As long as this owner was in this situation, he would not be able to grow effectively. Yet, he thought he could grow his way out of his existing troubles. Unfortunately, this wasn't the case. He ended up selling his business to one of his salespeople who, with the help of family members, invested in improvements to the equipment so that the job could be done properly and reliably each time. Then, with an increased focus on keeping promises, the business started to regain the customer loyalty it had lost.

Going for growth when you are not delivering on customer promises at your current size just makes for bigger messes. Your sales and marketing efforts will be lost if your ***lack of delivery capacity*** just alienates you to these new customers. It doesn't take long to ruin your reputation throughout a marketplace.

A better approach is to check in on your customer experience of value before adding to your sales and marketing efforts. Here are five questions to help you clarify how well you are doing:

1. Do you ask your customers how well you are doing on a regular, programmed basis? Customer satisfaction surveys are very useful for gaining feedback. People usually don't like doing surveys, but there is one exception to that rule: When you, as their existing supplier or service provider, check in to see how well you are serving them, people are actually glad to provide feedback.

2. When you ask your customers, do you confirm that the end result was achieved, and what their experience was like along the way? Many companies are focused on the end result, but ignore how their customers are treated in the meantime. Their experience of value starts when you start doing business with them, and doesn't finish until the job is done. Not only do you need to deliver the results you promise, but you want to make it more enjoyable to work with you along the way so your customers will value your contributions more highly.

3. Do you make it easy for your customers to complain about — or praise — you and your people? Many small business owners are so busy running around trying to deliver to their customers that they haven't built a mechanism for customer feedback. People usually feel good about sharing the good stuff, but are far less comfortable letting you know if things go wrong, unless they go so badly that anger or frustration takes over. The number one reason that customers leave is poor listening. Sixty-eight percent of all lost business has been attributed to that one fact alone. If people feel that either you or your staff are not listening, they don't usually make a big fuss. "What's the point?" they wonder. "You are not listening anyway!" So they just leave.

4. Do you track repeat sales and referrals in your business as a percentage of total business gained, and compare that to previous years? By doing this, you will pick up if your ratios start to slip and you can then check to see if you have a customer service problem. People will continue to buy from you until they find

an alternative, but they won't refer others to you if they are not happy. As soon as they have an alternative, they will take it.

5. Do you periodically send in a secret shopper to see what it is like to deal with your company? This is one way to check on the customer experience of value. The feedback from a "plant" will often give you a much better idea of your customer's experience. This person will know what to look for, and is being paid to identify the potential areas of vulnerability you may have, but which you may be unaware of within your own system. This feedback can be invaluable.

By checking in on the customer's experience before starting to scale, you will save yourself a great deal of dissipated effort, wheel spinning and lost profits. If the experience is not what you would like it to be, address that first. Tighten things up before you grow significantly. You will be glad you did!

Recap: *If you cannot deliver value to your customers at your current size, increasing the size of the company will likely cause more harm than good. If you can deliver measurable value, then growth becomes exciting.*

2. The Market Check

Do you have a market that will allow for desired levels of growth in the company?

One of the ingredients necessary to achieve large-scale growth is a marketplace big enough to tap in order to increase sales and customers.

Is your marketplace big enough to sustain a five- or ten-fold increase in your business? If you have 80% of the business in a particular area already, then you cannot double — at least not in that area. There just are not enough customers to allow for this kind of expansion.

For most small businesses in urban areas, this is not a problem as they are small in relation to the area's population. For businesses in rural areas, however, as well as for really unique specialty companies, this may pose a problem.

We have one client who provides engineering services to owners and operators of major sub-stations and refineries in his area. He doesn't really want to travel too far (not beyond a couple of hours' driving, unless it is for a one-time deal with an existing client), so he really is restricted to the client work he can gain from the dozen or so major potential customers in his vicinity. Even with that, he has been able to increase his professional services business to bring in almost triple what he was being paid previously as a senior-level employee in someone else's company.

Yet he is clear that he will never own a multi-million-dollar business. The professional practice he has feeds him and his wife and family and allows them to have the lifestyle they desire and provides him with funding for his eventual retirement. If he wanted to expand big time, it would mean going farther out geographically, and that would change the family lifestyle too much for his liking.

If you are dealing with a market segment that is very small, here are a few questions to ask yourself:

1. Is there enough business to allow you to sustain major changes in sales? Are there enough customers there for you to gain your share? Remember, there need to be enough customers and clients so that you don't have to have every single one to be successful. It is very hard work for everyone, unless you have a monopoly-type product that everyone needs and a competitor can't produce or sell in your area (very rare, but it does happen). You need to

leave room to allow for the fact that there will be some clients and customers you never get to deal with. An important thing to remember is that even though a geographic area may be small, that doesn't mean you can't grow. One of the greatest insurance salesmen in the United States, Ben Feldman, sold millions of dollars' worth of insurance in a small town of forty-thousand people. That was back in the days when a million was a big number, and the levels of sales he achieved were almost unheard of elsewhere.

2. If you don't think the market is large enough where you currently operate, then is geographic expansion a possibility? What will that do to your plans? Will a geographic expansion allow you to achieve your goals and wishes for how you want to run your business, and not just bring the end result of that growth – more sales? Sometimes it is easy to grow geographically, and at other times that may generate stresses that people just don't expect. What will the impact be on your lifestyle? Remember to check all your goals and commitments as you devise strategies so as to confirm your plans serve them all.

3. What is the possibility of expansion to different market or industry sectors? Two clients, a pair of process consultants to large businesses in telecommunications, found that their work could be converted for use by most types of small businesses, not just those in the telecommunications industry. As a result, they were quite successful at expanding their business by attending to these newly identified sectors of smaller customers.

By checking in advance to ensure that you have the market size available to grow into, you will be that much more prepared to seek and gain large-scale growth for your business, in service of your goals and commitments in life.

Recap: *If you already have 80% of the marketplace, it will be difficult to double your size in that market. Is the market you are serving large enough to support your company at the desired larger level? If not, are there other markets that are logical to target for expansion? If not, are there other products or services that your company might provide that will allow you to grow? These are all points for consideration when seeking to grow.*

3. The Resource Check

Do you have access to the resources needed to scale the company?

In most businesses there exists this thing called a choke point. That is, the limiting factor or resource that will impact the profitable growth of a company. If you can own your choke point, you are set. If it lies within someone else's control, then your business may be more vulnerable than you'd like.

One area to explore when considering substantial growth is the availability of all the resources you will need to accomplish your goals. Do you have easy access to what you will need to grow?

This leads to the question of what are the resources you will need. We had one potential client approach us looking to grow past his current limits within his business. He ran a very successful notary public office in British Columbia, Canada. As a notary, he was generating over $500,000 in gross revenues, almost double what most other notaries were making at the time. Yet he was stuck. He wanted to achieve significant growth, and free himself up from always needing to be available to notarize documents.

Here is where we ran into a problem. British Columbia is unique in that the notary business is regulated, with only a limited number of notary seals authorized. There can be no more. Further, all the authorized seals were out and in use by other notaries, who each had their own small practice. As a result, we saw no way that he could hire more notaries to provide the services he offered. He was left with the choices of either continuing the way he had been or to change his business model.

What he did was to add a separate business unit that provided packaged offices to solo entrepreneurs who needed space. This business, which was not regulated, had lots of upside for growth and expansion. He has since reduced his work as a notary, and now has a thriving business supplying small businesses and individual practitioners with office and other related services.

Another client, who owned a small chain of physical therapy clinics in the Greater Vancouver area, found it almost impossible to attract high-quality physical therapists to two of his locations in a distant suburb of town (forty miles from downtown, in a bedroom community). This turned out to be his choke point. After a few years of trying to get and keep good staff, he finally sold his business and opened up in a more central location, where he has no trouble finding great staff. The purchaser, on the other hand, continually fights with the same issue of trying to find good people who want to work in this bedroom community.

Special Note

Tight staffing is a problem for many businesses. Don't give up too easily. Excellent businesses can still hire good staff in tight labor markets. However, this takes strategizing and sorting out before you go too far. What else can you offer to the people you need to grow? Can you contact them personally? How can you make your recruiting process like your sales process? What kind of development/training process do you have? The situation involving the physical therapy office I mentioned was a little different from normal. Even though good physical therapists are hard to find in general, by moving to a geographic area that was more appealing to these young professionals, the owner was able to overcome his difficulty and continue his growth.

What is the limiting resource for you? By clarifying this in advance of seeking to grow, you may find that you can either confirm you are fine, or deal with the realities of the situation. Either way, you will be better prepared to take the steps necessary in moving toward your goals.

Recap: *Identify your choke point and get clear on what resources you will need to overcome it as you grow. Many entrepreneurs are unsure of where to look for the weak links in their organization's resources, and have developed a functional blindness to their own limitations. But the solutions are often nearer than they think.*

4. Respect for People

Do you have a core level of respect for people?

There are a number of beliefs and attitudes about people that you will need to generate and sustain large-scale growth. First and foremost is a core level of respect for people.

What is your fundamental belief about people? Is it limiting or negative? Nobody I have ever met believes that their perspective is negative. However, ask yourself these three questions:

1. Do you worry that others are just out to take from you, and get what they can?
2. Do you spend much of your time protecting yourself from others because it is a dog-eat-dog world out there?
3. Do you believe that the people aren't what matters, and it's the system that counts?

If any of these apply to you, don't even try large-scale growth without at least concurrently addressing these attitudes. It will be too hard. Your limiting beliefs will get in your way and make it more difficult for you to get what you need in order for your business to grow.

You see, whether you believe that the world is a wonderful place or that the world is dark and scary, you are correct.

Our beliefs become the lenses through which we see everything in life. If I believe that the world is bad, and that people are bad and cannot be trusted (and don't deserve my respect), then that will color what I see. I will notice anything that is not quite right, and I will likely miss the good stuff or dismiss it as a fluke.

On the other hand, if I believe that people are good, deserve my respect and are fundamentally interested in contributing to others, then I will notice the good that they do, and once again I will be proven correct.

If you have fears and concerns about people, or even disdain for people, then this will have a very large and negative impact on your ability to work with others (both staff and customers) to grow your business in a big way.

Recap: *Significant growth occurs with and through other people. Without a core level of respect for people, it just won't work.*

5. Contributing to Others

Do you have a fundamental desire to contribute significantly to others?

In addition to having a fundamental level of respect for people, I have found that large-scale growth is more readily available when you are actively interested in contributing significantly to other people, and combine that with an active interest in contributing significantly to yourself.

I believe that everyone has an inherent desire to contribute to other people. When that does not seem to be present, it is due to a scarcity mentality — there doesn't seem to be enough to go around, so you think you have to grab your share. This scarcity mentality is based in our survival instinct. It can be debilitating, as you miss many opportunities that you don't notice because you are busy chasing what feels like very few resources.

That is quite common for people to experience when they are stretched, or put into a new circumstance that requires more than they generated before. "How can I possibly worry about contributing to other people? I have to do everything I can to take care of myself!"

What you would miss if you thought the notion above is that there is real power in contributing to others. Your self-care is a whole different story, but you are capable of handling both. This is not a "me versus them" thing, but rather an integrative phenomenon.

If you have a fundamental interest and desire to conduct your activities in a manner that also supports others, then you will find it much easier to grow your business. In my research, an environment of mutual support seems to be the most productive, and is far more enjoyable, too!

Recap: *If you are not interested in serving others, my experience is that it will be very difficult (and unrewarding) for you to maintain the experience of value to customers and staff. If you are committed to contribution, then growth can be a lot easier, and a lot of fun, too!*

6. Contributing to Yourself

Do you have a fundamental desire to contribute significantly to *yourself?*

If you are just out to serve others, there is a risk that your service will come at your expense if you don't have an equal interest in serving and supporting yourself.

Those who spend their lives giving of themselves to others are very noble people usually referred to as martyrs. There is only one problem with this: martyrs, by definition, are dead. They give of themselves in service to others, and at some point, they wear out or come to some other unfortunate end.

If you become worn out from helping other people, you will not be able to sustain any gains you have made, and you risk losing any growth you do manage to achieve.

The best thing you can do for others is to exercise self-care along the way. This may take any number of forms, but it is always essential.

The bigger the game of business becomes, the more important it is for you to take good care of yourself. The larger the business, the more you are paid to **think**, and the less you are paid to do. If self-care is not actively present, then you are just dwarfing your future ability to continue what you started, which includes helping and supporting others.

This tendency to take care of others at our own expense is very common and will eventually sink a growing business. Its consequences can be dire. The first thing to go, if you are not supporting yourself adequately, is your trust in your own decisions. If you start to doubt yourself, then your confidence erodes. We all know that people are more effective when confidence is higher and less effective when confidence is lower and self-doubt creeps in.

One area this shows up in is pricing — caving in and providing discounts that, when you are feeling confident, you would know you don't need to give, thus eroding your margin and hurting your profits. That doesn't mean you should never provide a discount. However, when you are taking good care of yourself and trusting your own instincts, you are in a much better position to determine when discounts are appropriate, and what discounts (if any) to give in a particular situation.

A few questions to ask yourself: Do you undercharge for your services? Do you know when you need to charge more, but don't? Do you give your staff or suppliers excessive latitude when you know it will hurt your business? This business thing really is a balancing act. You need all your wits about you.

That is why self-care is so important. The bigger you get, the more important this will become.

Recap: *Contributing to others is not sufficient. There are enough martyrs around who wear themselves out and use themselves up helping others. If you want to contribute significantly to yourself while contributing to others, then you maintain balance in relationships and growth comes much easier.*

7. The Power of People

Do you have a belief in the power of people to achieve extraordinary things in life?

Another belief that impacts your ability to grow big is your belief (or lack of belief) in the power of people. Some entrepreneurs do very well up to a certain point (usually at ten employees) and then seem to plateau at that level. Here is a question to ask yourself: When you see people, do you see their strengths and potential first, or do you see their limitations?

If you first see their limitations, this may become tough sledding for you if you try to grow too big too quickly. If you see people's limits, that is what will show up. There is another possibility, however. If you see their potential, things shift.

By nurturing other people's potential, combined with helping them to access their inspiration, people are capable of amazing things. There are companies out there who continue to stymie their competitors by achieving truly unbelievable goals using fewer resources than others think possible. Nobody can figure out what it is about these companies that is so special.

Well, there is a lot going on in these companies, but none of what the owners do and/or encourage would make a difference if they didn't also believe in the power of people to perform at these higher levels. What you expect, you will get.

Believe in the power of people to accomplish extraordinary things in life. You may need people to do just that in order to meet your goals. If you believe in people's ability to stretch and grow to meet larger objectives, magic can occur.

Recap: *If you believe in (and tap) the power of people, you will find the task of achieving large-scale growth for your business that much easier. This thinking will serve you well as you seek to grow your business in support of your goals.*

8. Gaining Input and Challenging the Norm

Are you open to outside input? Do you have a willingness to try new things and to challenge conventional norms?

No one who achieves financial success gets there based solely upon what they already knew. The ability to utilize outside resources and to integrate them into your own business practices is essential to growing your business.

Entrepreneurs explore a variety of strategies when faced with difficult challenges, but those who are open to outside help, try creative approaches and experiment with unconventional solutions are more likely to thrive in a competitive environment.

Your ability to re-evaluate and reframe how you see and operate your business often depends on how well you are able to listen to, nurture and implement outside support. Try meeting with people from different companies or industries and see what challenges they face and how they overcome them. Chances are you'll be able to learn something about running your business in the process because you will have examined it from a different perspective.

The more you learn about which resources might work for you, the better you will be at identifying the ones that meet your needs. If you are unwilling to listen to advice from others with an open mind, you will invariably be faced with challenges that are beyond your ability to solve, and you will get stuck.

Recap: Are you hungry to draw on the multitude of resources that are available to you? Are you willing to step outside the box, to challenge conventional norms and to try something new in order to transform your business? If so, you are well on your way to achieving large-scale growth in your business.

9. The Growth Check

Do you have a willingness to do what it takes to grow, including potentially uncomfortable shifts if appropriate?

Large-Scale growth is more available to business owners than many people realize. Too often, we see our constraints and limitations rather than seeing what is possible to us from growing our business big time.

WHAT STOPS US?

There are three main factors (or perceptions) that stop people from taking on large-scale growth:

1. Lack of Knowledge
2. Lack of Confidence
3. A Perceived Lack of Money

One (or more) of these three issues will have a bigger negative impact, and keep entrepreneurs stuck at their current level, than any other factors that business owners face.

On many occasions I have heard people say, "I just don't know how to grow my business much bigger without killing myself! It is already wearing me out just to get it to this level. I don't know how!" Others say, "I know how, but I am afraid to try taking it on. What if my business self-destructs while I am in the middle of my growth plans?" And still other people say, "I know how, and I am not afraid. I just don't have the money to fund what I want."

If these three walls can be overcome, then the task becomes much easier to accomplish, and far more predictable, too.

LACK OF KNOWLEDGE (AND CONFIDENCE)

One of the most significant barriers entrepreneurs face is that they just don't know how to grow big without wearing themselves out in the process. They know what it took to get to where they are, and they didn't expect it to be so hard. As a result, getting to the next level must be more grinding, tiring and time-consuming, right? If this is true, then they see no way to grow without killing themselves in the process.

Of course, if you are missing knowledge, you must fill in the gaps through learning. We all know that there are many ways to learn, so let's review a few of these ways:

School

Going to school has always been the most accepted form of learning. Yet, what do they teach at school? I went through the commerce program in my undergraduate studies, and then took my MBA at the graduate level, and I must admit I never did see a course on How to Make a Lot of Money 101 or How to Grow Big from Small 202. This was true at both institutions I attended.

Further, I have yet to see these types of practical courses offered anywhere in the school system. Even entrepreneurial studies programs, which are sprouting up in some of the university MBA programs, are trying to teach business from a textbook, and the practical application just doesn't seem to be there.

Books

Much has been written on business and business growth. The book in your hands is one example of this. And much of what has been written is very good. If you can cull from all the different versions of what to do and how to do it, you will be able to stitch together something that might work. While it is possible to gain the right knowledge to grow the way you want to, how likely is it that you will succeed? It sounds like a difficult process to me.

Home Study Courses

Using this method of learning is better than reading mere books, as it taps the various senses. There is usually a manual, some audio CDs, and possibly even a DVD or two offered with these courses. By providing people with the information in a number of different formats, learning can be customized to suit the learner. In addition, CDs may be used to make non-productive time more productive. For example, your commute (whether it's drive time, time in planes or on public transit) is a time when you do nothing except perhaps listen to tunes on the way to and from work. If you listen to CDs, your time becomes more productive. With a half hour commute to work, you have a total of five hours of potential listening time (there and back each day, all week) that can be used to learn more. Further, you can listen to one or more segments again and again and again until you really internalize the information you want. However, while this is better than merely using written material, it is not the complete answer either. Too often, such materials sit on a shelf and people don't seem to get the work done, given their busy lives and busy businesses.

Live Seminars and Workshops

These events seem to be even more effective than home study courses. In a two-, three- or four-day event, you sit through the entire proceeding from start to finish so you gain the full picture from the wisdom of others who have been there and have done it. This immersion method leaves people with a full and complete picture, rather than the incomplete one you get from programs that you never complete. Further, you can get your questions answered and clear up any sources of confusion that might arise. Yet these are not fool-proof either. Have you ever left a seminar all pumped up and encouraged, only to find that your memory faded over the ensuing weeks and months (or even days)?

I recently heard about a couple of master's-level students who did a longitudinal study on the effectiveness of various learning methods on the students' success in learning the material, and on the effectiveness of using new knowledge in a new business. The statistics they unearthed were very revealing. They found that the success rates of various methods of learning were as follows:

- Written materials alone – 5% of the people succeeded or reached their goal using this method
- Home study courses – 10% succeeded using this method
- Seminar training – 21% of the people studied were successful using this mode of learning

The study went on to list a few other areas, but did not include direct experience (or trial and error). Direct experience is a curious method of learning, as most who just use that method find out more about what doesn't work than about what does.

None of the learning methods guaranteed success, except for one. That was apprenticeship with a true craftsman. This method (at least according to this one study) brought 100% success.

Craftsman and Apprentice

There were a number of things the students found unique about the craftsmen followed in their study. They found that craftsmen pick their apprentices, and would not work with someone unless the elder believed that the candidate had true potential to be successful in the chosen field. Then, the craftsman would work directly with the junior, showing the things that work in the field, rather than wasting time with what things don't work.

There were four stages to an apprentice's growth. Ignorance was the first stage. The apprentice had to gain clarity on how little he/she knew. Only an empty cup may be filled. The second stage was awareness. Once open to what the master had to offer, real learning started to occur. The craftsman would tell the apprentice the correct way to do things, and then the apprentice would be shown as well.

This led to the third stage, where the apprentice tried it. By applying what was being taught, the apprentice was being told, then shown, and then was doing it. Then, when a procedure was sufficiently understood, the fourth stage was applied — practice. The apprentice practiced this skill or procedure until it was second nature.

Using discernment during the selection process, combined with these four stages of teaching, craftsmen were consistently able to support their apprentices in reaching their goals successfully. Then, lack of money ceased being an issue as well, but was rather just another logistic to address in the development of the business.

Recap: *Whether it is through trial and error, reading, home study courses, seminars or mentoring from a master, any properly applied knowledge you gain will help you to achieve your business objectives and grow your business consistent with your goals and commitments in life.*

10. The Strategic Check

Are you committed to staying strategic and do you trust your abilities?

Growing your company means that you will inevitably have to stretch and grow yourself. What many small business owners don't realize is that many of the limitations we experience are actually self-imposed. It takes a willingness to grow personally and professionally to sustain major changes.

Almost anyone can have a one-time leap in revenue. Ongoing increases in revenue require that you learn and grow alongside your company. This period of growth may be uncomfortable at times, so if you are not willing to do what it takes, large-scale growth may not be a good idea. Think about people who squander their lottery winnings: more often than not, such winners didn't grow to meet the challenges of handling their new-found wealth.

Life will shift fairly dramatically as you grow, and what may be working for you now may well become a limitation in a significantly larger company. If you enjoy discovering your limits and working past them, then personal and professional growth is within your reach.

Due to the nature of the shifts involved, a continued focus on the larger strategy makes a huge difference on both your effectiveness and your success. Staying strategic makes it easier as well.

Recap: *If you trust yourself to act consistent with your core values and beliefs, and to do what makes sense to you, the road will be much smoother, and difficult decisions will become easier to make and to implement. This is your business. Make sure that it serves your goals and commitments in your life. This element allows you to maintain perspective, which will serve you well as you grow.*

CHAPTER 3

Take Time Off

Take Time Off

Large-Scale growth is not easy to achieve. You can attain it by following the steps within this book, but to attempt this, you must be well-rested. It is incredible how many people try to operate without adequate self-care. Nothing will harm your plans to grow more than trying to get things done without all of your personal resources directly at hand – including all of your energy.

If you have grown a business to your target size (say ten times the size of your current business) in the past and sold it, then you know what I mean. However, if you haven't done this before, you will be in uncharted territory. You really will need all of your faculties in their best working order before you go through the learning curve you are about to experience.

The biggest threat to small business is time. There seems to be too much to do and too little of you to get it all done! Yet, growing a business isn't about getting more done, at least not directly. As I mentioned earlier, the bigger a company gets, the more you are paid to think and the less you are paid to do. This usually sounds contrary to what we expect to hear. After all, we have been raised with the notion that lots of hard work and a little luck will be all it takes to succeed in life. That may be true of many things, but it definitely does NOT apply to the large-scale growth of a business.

People are very familiar with the traditional model of time at work — you know, where you work Monday through Friday and take the weekends off as a reward for the time spent at work. There's only one problem with this for the entrepreneur: Are you paid for your time, or are you paid for your results in your business?

If you are like the many entrepreneurs I know, you are paid for your results, NOT your time. Results are stronger and confidence levels are higher when you are rested. Even if you bill clients on an hourly basis, growing your business is about the results you generate, not just your billable time.

The Three Zones

Let's look at the traditional work week from a different perspective: If you put Saturday and Sunday at the start of your week, using those days to rest and rejuvenate, then when it is time to return to work, you will be fresher, more relaxed, more centered and balanced. This is only true if you use the weekend to support your self-care. Better still, let's say you just had one or two weeks off and you are coming back to work fresh. Then, when you go to work on Monday, you enter into the first of three distinct zones of effectiveness:

ZONE ONE: CLARITY AND CREATIVITY

The first zone you will enter is what I call the Clarity and Creativity Zone. This occurs when your thinking is the clearest. When your confidence is high, you bring real certainty to the situation at hand. You are on top of your game. This is when really productive brainstorming can occur, and new initiatives (or new solutions to previous problems) unfold. The productive thinking done in this first zone leads to the second.

ZONE TWO: TASK ACCOMPLISHMENT

The second zone is the Task Accomplishment Zone. With all the clarity that you have and the creativity that you tap, you come up with great ideas and solutions. Now is time to do something with them. Life rewards action, so you get into action. You start tackling those issues and tapping those opportunities. This zone, like the first, is also a very productive one. However, it eventually leads to the third, more difficult zone.

ZONE THREE: PROBLEMS

The third zone is the Problem Zone. As your energy starts to wane and you get tired, you start encountering more problems. Your effectiveness drops and it doesn't quite feel the same as when you first took on tasks or thought through problems. This zone is encountered by everyone. Some just don't recognize it; others (especially you adrenaline junkies) won't admit it. But whether you admit it or not doesn't change whether it exists. It is very real. When we are fatigued or tired or worn down, we tend to take a little longer to accomplish the same things, or else we take shortcuts or make mistakes. The problems are more plentiful and the road is a little more difficult to travel.

The Key

The secret to increased effectiveness is to take more time off between Zone Two and Zone Three. If you take time for yourself before you get tired, you will go back to the Clarity and Creativity Zone, where issues may be thought through and resolved more easily, and where your confidence will support increased momentum as you move into the second zone again.

The Hidden Dynamic with Fatigue

The problem with getting tired (or becoming mentally fatigued by a situation) is that the first thing affected is our self-trust; we start to second-guess ourselves when we wear down. This impacts our confidence levels.

Just ask yourself: When your confidence is high, how effective are you? If you are like most people I ask, the answer will be "very effective". However, when your confidence is low, and you are second-guessing yourself, how effective are you? The answer will most likely be "less effective".

Your confidence level has a direct impact on your personal effectiveness. Your level of rest or fatigue has a direct impact on your confidence. This is the hidden link that most people don't realize. Self-care is critical if you want to grow your business multifold.

> ***The bigger your business is, the less you are paid to DO, and the more you are paid to THINK.***

- What are some of the areas that directly impact your personal energy levels?
- Amount of sleep?
- Time away from work?
- Eating right?
- Time away from work?
- Personal space?
- Time away from work?
- Exercise and fitness level?

Did I mention time away from work?

My Personal Story

Back in 1996, one year after I started Kaizen Consulting, my wife and I had not taken a vacation for three years. We planned a trip to Mexico, just the two of us. My brother David was going to fly to Vancouver (where we live) to take care of Kathleen, our daughter, who was four years old at the time. Well, David got sick and couldn't come to care for Kathleen. My wife suggested I go anyway, alone, telling me I really needed the break.

This felt weird. Going to Mexico alone? I had never taken a vacation or time off alone before. I was really having a difficult time rationalizing this, even though my wife was clear that this was what I needed. I came up with something I could live with. People go away to conferences all the time. I just didn't know of any conferences for small business consultants, so I held my own conference!

I brought a bulky three-inch binder containing a full system on how to do customer satisfaction surveys. I decided that I would become familiar with this whole process, which I had wanted to learn about but never had any time to address.

For the first three days in Mexico I just slept — literally. I didn't realize how tired I was until I stopped long enough to catch up with myself. On about day four I started coming to life and decided that I had better get started on the task at hand. I brought the big binder down to the pool and read it, clad in my bathing suit, a T-shirt, and my Vancouver Canucks ball hat. About every forty-five minutes or so I would jump into the pool and have a little swim, and then set about reading some more. Despite my initial warped sense of what a vacation was, I found myself getting some much-needed rest. I felt so rejuvenated after the time off that I came home and sold four different clients the service of conducting customer satisfaction surveys for them, an activity that paid me tens of thousands of extra dollars, and served my clients even more!

I really liked this idea of time off — so much so that in the next fifteen months, I took eight weeks off, one week at a time. Within six months of starting this, my income rose by over 40%. Even though I was spending less time on client work, my revenues were higher because my effectiveness was much improved. I found that the more rested I was, the easier it became for me to help my clients. This surprised me, as up until then I had been very effective at work, and I honestly didn't think I was tired.

In January of 1998, I decided that I needed to formally structure time off into my regular routine. I needed a rationalization to satisfy my mind (we humans are amazing creatures, aren't we?), and I found one: Teachers get twelve weeks off a year. They get nine weeks in the summer, two weeks at Christmas and a week at spring break. While I know that teachers are important, taking care of our youth, I decided that I worked just as hard as a teacher and should get that much time off as well. I couldn't take nine weeks off at once (the clients would leave, I feared). But I had just demonstrated to myself that I could take a week off whenever I wanted. So I decided to take off the last week of every month, for a total of twelve weeks per year. I have been taking at least twelve weeks off each year since 1998.

Now I am up to seventeen to eighteen weeks off per year, which totals about four months out of twelve. I take either one or two weeks off at the end of each month. I often look to see what conferences exist during these times, or what interesting places I might visit. What I notice now is that if I miss taking time off, I get tired and cranky and the people around me notice and point it out to me. In the meantime, things continue to build and grow in our company.

Now, some people argue this point, saying that they are effective just the way they are. That's fine. Take a look at how effective you are. No matter how great things are for you (and I have no doubt that they are, in fact, great—they were for me too), just think how much better you would be if you got more rest!

By focusing on taking care of the goose who lays the golden eggs, rather than working that goose to exhaustion, you will find that this journey of growth will be much more rewarding and enjoyable.

Steps for Taking Time Off

For those of you who are wondering how to accomplish this task of taking time off, here are the four steps to take:

Step 1. Decide how much time off you want this coming year. You may not decide to take twelve weeks, but I recommend at least four

weeks off—one week each quarter. Remember that the goal here is to get yourself rested, and a week each quarter will allow you to go strong for twelve weeks and then catch up, so you can do it all again.
Step 2. Take out your Daytimer.
Step 3. Schedule the time in your Daytimer.
Step 4. Follow your Daytimer.

That's it. Yes, it is that simple. We make it far more complicated than it really is. Just book the time off and take it. End of story.

Here are a few safety tips to help you with this shift in both perspective and action:

Safety Tips

1. You might want to book time away (that is, go somewhere instead of staying at home). I tried to take time off while staying at home, and found that it just didn't work. People found me, and I had a hard time telling them, "No, I will not help you." So I went away. Clients and customers seem to understand your need for time off better when you physically go away.

2. Tell the people around you that you will not be around, and make alternative arrangements for problems and issues to be handled (i.e. other than through you). By setting things up beforehand, you will find that others will handle the issues you are normally needed for. This is important to know when you grow your business, as these are some of the very issues that are keeping you from growing in the first place.

3. When taking time off, don't call the office. If you call, you are looking for problems, and you will find them.

4. You will need to free up your time in order to grow your business. If you are unable or unwilling to take off four full weeks in a year (one week at a time), I recommend against taking on large-scale growth for your business. Some of the other things you will need to accomplish to achieve large-scale growth are much more difficult than this step, so if you can't take time off, you will never achieve the growth you want.

5. Don't be surprised if you come back to a few problems when you first start taking time off. Instead of regretting leaving, treat this as good information. The areas where there are problems are areas where you are under-structured in your business. These areas will need to be addressed in order for you to grow.

    By taking on these problems one at a time, you will discover that by the time you are on your fourth or fifth week-long holiday, many or most of them will have been solved. You won't continue to leave without handling these issues first, so by organizing for your absence, you are also preparing the underlying structures for the growth of your business. Remember, if you can't be replaced, you can't be promoted, and that includes being promoted to running your future bigger company as it grows.

6. Don't accept a drop in income as a way of achieving this time-off goal. Anyone can take time off by merely working part-time and making less. The key is to take more time off while earning more in the process. That makes it far more interesting. Besides, you will need more money for all those vacations!

Take this one step at a time, consistent with the notion of kaizen. By taking one week off, and then trying it again, you will be able to identify the structures that you need to address. You will also find yourself moving toward a much more satisfying lifestyle, and you will keep yourself well-rested enough to accomplish your goals for growth. Your overall business and personal goals will be well within your reach as a result.

Exercise: Time Off

1. a) How much time did you say you were actually going to take off in each of the past two years?
   b) How much time did you actually take off?

   _____
   _____
   _____

2. In the past two years, how much of your time off was spent without being in contact with the office, or without checking email or voicemail?

   _____
   _____
   _____

3. How much time would you like to be taking off?

   _____
   _____
   _____

4. How much time will you be taking off in the next twelve months? List the weeks here, by date:

   _____
   _____
   _____

Risk-Managing Capacity

Related to the issue of taking time off is that of risk-managing your capacity levels. Have you ever seen very accomplished people start dropping the ball on the basics within their job? Ever wonder, "What happened to them?"

Quite often, these people are in a state called capacity overload. They are past the edges of their personal capacity levels. This can be particularly costly to the entrepreneur, on whose talents the business relies. Many businesses have been lost to capacity overload, and others have gone through severe setbacks because of it. This gets extremely expensive when an entrepreneur is going for large-scale growth.

This phenomenon occurs quite frequently when entrepreneurs do not manage their environment. It is also all too common when they are entering a new zone in their business—a game on a much larger scale. People do well when times are good, but do they have the capacity to handle things when times are stormy? How do you manage your affairs to minimize the disruptions that diminish your capacity? How do you risk manage your capacity while attempting large-scale growth?

Foundation

In business, it is essential to handle and maintain your foundation issues and items. Foundational items are those things in our lives that are invisible as long as they are working, but take an inordinate amount of effort to deal with when things go wrong.

One example of this is your computer system. Anyone who has had their computer crash without the hard drive backed up is painfully aware of the cost of this event, both in time and in heartache.

Computer crashes do occur, but the drain in energy of the "crashee" is inversely proportional to how recently the backup occurred (if at all!). Losing your work, such as important customer files or company product and financial information, may have a dramatic, negative effect on your business. Proper system maintenance, however, may reduce the incidence of crashes, and timely backups will certainly reduce the consequences.

Other examples include cars and babysitting. Have you ever had a mechanical breakdown on the freeway? Have you ever had a babysitter not show up or call in sick? These are but a few of the many things we routinely take for granted. They are invisible when they are working, but they take what feels like far too much energy to set right when they don't go as planned.

What are your foundation items? Identify them and maintain them while they still work. They will be tested as you grow. And be sure to build in a Plan B (and C and D if need be) just in case something does go wrong.

Personal Space

Another cause of diminished capacity is a lack of personal space. Similar to taking insufficient time off, entrepreneurs are notorious for spreading themselves too thin while helping, supporting and providing for others.

Newsflash: Your first commitment to your customers, your suppliers, your staff, and your family (yes, even your family!) is to stay sane enough to meet all those other commitments in life. Your capacity to handle commitments as you move out of your comfort zone is directly proportional to your physical and mental state.

For some people, personal space means going for a workout. For others it could mean eating ice cream while walking in the park on a sunny afternoon. The important thing is not what you do so much as whether or not your rejuvenation time actually rejuvenates you.

New moms seem to lose their personal space with the birth of a child. New business owners often lose this space as well. Entrepreneurs are paid for results, not for their inputs. The fresher you are, the faster you will see results. Mistakes caused by fatigue cost lots of time. How much more effective might you be if you carved out a little more time for yourself on a regular basis?

What do you do to ensure that you give yourself adequate personal space? Is it enough for you? If your answer includes some element of "It's all that is available to me," then you probably need to increase the time available to rejuvenate you. We often have more control than we give ourselves credit for.

If you can't take care of yourself, how are you going to grow your business as big as you want, to meet your goals and commitments in life? It just makes no sense.

Personal Money

It seems that very little drains capacity levels more than stress over money. People spend a great deal of time and energy worrying about their money. Furthermore, shortcuts are often taken when funds are tight—shortcuts that usually create problems down the road.

Taking the wrong customers is a good example of this. If your car is on the end of the repossessor's hook and you are eating Wheaties for dinner with water (because you just can't quite afford the milk) then you are far more likely to take a new customer that you know will later cause you anguish and grief (a PITA, which is a technical term for "Pain in the Assets"). This will strain your capacity levels in the future, not to mention the constant distraction of financial concerns in the meantime.

As an alternative, what if you had TBM? TBM is another technical term. It stands for "Talking Back Money". Would you take on a PITA customer if your bills were all paid and you had a bunch of extra money in the bank? Might there be a little more freedom available?

"Yes, that's nice, but how do you build these types and levels of reserves?" The time to sort this one out is now. Not when you have more money, or when you get that next big deal, but now. Many financial planners talk about setting aside 10% of your income to build a buffer or a reserve. Others will argue that it is better to pay down debt (at a higher interest rate) than save money. However, there is a problem with the "debt repayment first, no matter what" logic. It ignores our humanity. Please allow me to explain.

Some people pour all of their efforts into paying down debt, sometimes over a long period of time (many months to many years). After all this effort to pay off debt, they feel they deserve a reward—and they do! It is hard to maintain the discipline to pay off large debt loads. So what do they do? They celebrate and treat themselves, going into debt again. And the cycle continues…

What if you got into the habit of saving some money even as you chipped away at debt? It might take you longer to pay down the debt, but after you are done, you will have money stored up, and a solid habit as well. If you wanted to treat yourself at this point, you would not need to go into debt to do so.

Becoming A Millionaire

Here is how to become a cash millionaire:
- Start by putting $50,000 in the bank (cash money, not borrowed).
- What if you don't have $50,000 to do this? The first step to putting $50,000 in the bank is to put $10,000 in the bank.
- The first step to putting $10,000 in the bank is to put $1,000 in the bank. This breaks down to $83.33 per month.
- If $83.33 per month is too much, then how about $10 per month?

If $10 per month is too much, stop worrying about how to become a millionaire and get to work on your business. For the rest of us, why not start today? Developing the habit is the first and most important step. By handling our personal money, we are freed up to use our creativity to deal more effectively with the business, leaving fewer potential problems to challenge our capacity levels.

Your Access to Money

Some people continually feel frustrated and lose energy over having insufficient funds to achieve their goals, or their lack of access to money. Someone once asked me, "Does it take money to make money?" The answer to that question is usually a clear and definitive "yes".

However, it doesn't have to be YOUR money. Some people ask Mom or Dad; others go to other family and/or friends. Still others go to the bank. If you were charged 6% for the use of someone else's money, and you knew you could gain a 100% return, would it make financial sense to do it? For most people the answer would be yes, as long as the risk of loss was well managed. What if it cost 12%? Same answer – as long as the risk of loss was managed, then most people would go ahead and pay a small amount of interest to gain a big return. What if the cost of borrowing was 30% (such as a credit card) and the return was still 100%? The answer would be the same as it was for the first two questions.

Well, for many people, borrowing money to buy inventory to resell to a waiting list of customers is one scenario (based upon a 100% mark-up) comparable to the one I listed above. In a growing business, there are many examples of how funds are used to pay an owner a very high return.

If you are concerned about your money, list all the places you could go to access funds if the right opportunity came along, the return was high enough, and the risks managed. Remember, the key here is to make sure you are handling the risks associated with any such investment – in your business or anywhere. However, if you knew it was a good (and safe) deal, where would you go for funds? Make a list of these sources.

I am not suggesting that you run out and max out all your credit cards. However, I am recommending that you always keep that list of potential sources of funds updated and current, and add to it regularly. Further, you may want to nurture the relationships with any people on that list, be it your banker or that rich uncle. Generating the list of potential financial resources may be one of the most important exercises you conduct to maintain perspective and avoid worry about money.

Bonus: The Capacity Protector™

If you want to identify what (specifically) is diminishing your capacity, you may want to use this process. Look to see where your energy is going. To do this, simply list all the things you should have already done that you have not completed yet. Please exclude from this list those items that you are currently working on, where you have not fallen behind. Just include those items where you have fallen behind.

Then, cross off those items that you know you will not do. Whether you think you "should" do them or not is immaterial. This is time for a reality check. For each item, if deep down you know you won't do it, then cross it off the list. Next, delegate those items that you can. Finally, start working through this list (starting with a few easy ones first, to get your confidence back up).

As you work through this list, you will find that you gain your energy back, which in turn may assist you in replenishing your capacity levels and your confidence.

By addressing and maintaining foundation items before they become a problem, and by giving yourself the personal space you need to be effective, and by building your TBM, you will risk manage your capacity levels. You will reduce the chances of, and the impact of, "Capacity Overload" as you grow your business. This will in turn have a positive impact on business profitability and your personal satisfaction.

CHAPTER 4

Free Yourself Up

Free Yourself Up

Anyone can talk about growing, but if you are already too busy maintaining your current business, when will you have the time to grow it? You need to free yourself up so that you will have the time to think through and implement your growth strategies. While that is easy to say, it can also be done.

The Importance of This Step

In almost every business I have had the privilege to help grow, the highest leverage asset of that business has been the owner. No matter what you are doing now, there are tasks you are accomplishing that other less expensive people could do—quite often better than you could!

Many people get stuck by trying to save money through doing things themselves. What you don't realize is that your time is probably the most important resource your entire company has at its fingertips. But if you are spending a good chunk of your time handling the bookkeeping, for example, you won't have the time to deal with the larger aspects of growth. It is important when you are just starting out to survive. That's probably why you were doing the bookkeeping (or filing, or invoicing, or whatever) in the first place. However, others could do that job for between $15 and $40 per hour. If your time, freed up, is not worth more than that, perhaps you need to go into the bookkeeping business rather than the one you are currently operating. For the rest of us, get the bookkeeper (or file clerk, or assistant—you fill in the blank) to free up your time.

First Things First

Before you can free up your time, you need to figure out exactly what you do with your time each day and each week. Countless times when dealing with entrepreneurs, I come across the situation where the owners just aren't quite sure where their days go. People know that they are busy, but they spend so much time reacting to the issues that arise that they never get to their top priorities.

One of the templates at the end of this chapter is an Activity Inventory Template. This will assist you with seeing exactly how you spend your time each day. The time slots in the template start early in the morning and cover a full twenty-four hours. This is designed to catch everything you do, from the time you wake up in the morning until you go to sleep at night. Some people stop working when they leave the office; others don't stop until they drop into bed at night. Still others get up in the middle of the night and answer their email. By recording your own activities in detail for a week, you will gain a much better idea of exactly what your work patterns are and what fills up your days.

Instructions

1. Refer to the Activity Inventory Template at the end of this section. Print seven copies of this template, one for each of the next seven days.

   If you are very good at taking time off (for example, during the weekend), you may only need to do this for five days. If not, then take a look at your weekend activities as well. This is a good reality check, to see how much time you actually take off, as well as an inventory of the things you do for your business.

2. Starting with the first day, simply track what you do as you go. List the activity that you are doing for each time slot throughout the day. These templates are designed to be completed as your day develops. The more rigor you bring to this exercise, the more useful it will be to you. Leave the Ranking column until after you have gained the data from a full week's worth of activities. It will only get in your way if you start ranking as you go. After the week is done, rank your activities according to the ranking system provided with the Activity Inventory Template.

3. Next, refer to the Activity Ranking Template, also at the end of this section. Once you have all the data collected, follow the instructions at the bottom of the Activity Inventory Template, then transfer the information to the Activity Ranking Template. By listing your activities in each of the areas provided, you will see what has strategic significance for you, what you could delegate to others, and what wastes your time.

Delegation vs. Abdication

Some people think that dumping a task on another person is effective delegation. It is not. That is what we call abdication. You give a series of tasks to someone else, and then don't check in with them, hoping that they will get it done. You may even be a little afraid to check, in case they are not doing what you need, or doing it wrong – which means you will have to take back those activities again.

This is a very common experience for new delegators, as well as for avoiders. Sometimes it feels like you are getting someone else to do your dirty work for you (you know, the things you hate doing). You figure that if you hate doing that particular activity, then the person you assign this task to must hate it as well. If this is the case, you are probably doing it wrong. You want to give these activities to someone who is better at them than you are, and who enjoys doing them.

Take bookkeeping, for example. I have met many visionary business owners who hate the drudgery of bookkeeping. Then they feel bad about delegating this series of tasks to someone else. The key is to find someone who likes bookkeeping and invite them to do it. This way, you are not delegating downwards. You are actually delegating upwards, to someone who is better at this task than you are, who also enjoys it more than you.

Don't Have Someone To Delegate To?

Another very common problem that business owners face is that everyone on their team is already too busy. There is no additional bandwidth in anyone's schedule to take on your tasks. This means that it is time to hire someone new. I have found that one of the highest leverage positions available to facilitate growth in a company is to get the owner an administrative (or executive or personal) assistant. An assistant will free you up from lots of the legwork you may be doing now, so that you may focus on the higher leverage activities that will bring you more customers, profits and cash flow.

Can't afford this step? Well, think again. This is where the risk of growing comes into play. It is a risk to grow a business, and every new hire forms part of that risk. However, keep in mind that hiring a person to do the lower level activities that eat up your day will free you up to do more productive, and profitable things.

As the owner, you are the highest leverage person in your business. If you were freed up from the things that others could do just as well as or better than you for less money than you take, how would you reinvest your time? If the answer is that you would invest it in more lucrative activities, it may well be time to take this particular risk.

With your time freed up, you can generate more business, which will more than pay for the new person. That is how business grows.

Safety Tips

You may not be starting with an administrative assistant. Take a look through your activities ranking and see which lower paid role will give you the most of your time back, and start with that one.

When hiring someone new, look for the skills that are consistent with the role you seek to fill. Too often, owners hire others just like them, rather than people with complementary skills. No matter how much more easily you see eye-to-eye with the person with similar skills to you, it will probably be the one with the complementary skills who will serve you better.

To avoid hiring a clone of yourself (that is, someone with the same skills and weak spots as you), invite someone you trust to be there to assist you with the hiring process. This will increase the likelihood of finding someone who truly complements and supports you, rather than someone who is just like you.

If you take these steps to first identify how you are spending your time each day, and then start delegating tasks, you will start to free up the time that you will need to properly grow your business.

Activity Inventory and Ranking Templates

ACTIVITY INVENTORY TEMPLATE

TIME	ACTIVITY (Early Morning)	RANK

TIME	ACTIVITY (Morning)	RANK

TIME	ACTIVITY (Afternoon)	RANK

TIME	ACTIVITY (Evening)	RANK

TIME	ACTIVITY (Late Night)	RANK

RANKING SYSTEM

Go through the activities that you have just listed and assign a rank to each of them.

1a.	I am very good at and enjoy this, and it has high strategic value.
1b.	I am very good at this, and enjoy it, but others could do it just as well as me.
2.	I am very good at this, but I would rather not if I didn't have to.
3.	I am ok at this, but others could do it just as well or better than me.
4.	I only do this because I have to; I avoid it where possible; I'm no good at this.

Activities Ranking Template

1a.	I am very good at and enjoy this, and it has high strategic value.

1b.	I am very good at this, and enjoy it, but others could do it just as well as me.

2.	I am very good at this, but I would rather not, if I didn't have to.

3.	I am ok at this, but others could do it just as well or better than me.

4.	I only do this because I have to; I avoid it where possible; I'm no good at this.

CHAPTER 5

Set Your Target

Set Your Target

What Do You Want?

Achieving large-scale growth sounds like an exciting idea, but it also takes a lot of work. Why would you put yourself through all that? The fact is, you wouldn't unless it was worth it somehow.

A business is a tool that supports you in achieving something. Similarly, a stapler is a tool that helps keep papers together. A car is also a tool—it helps you to get from point A to point B. Some cars get you there in more style than others, and some are more comfortable than others. Yet at the end of the day, both staplers and cars are examples of tools that assist you in achieving what you want.

A business is a far more powerful tool than a stapler or a car, however. It is also far trickier than your stapler to operate. Similar to a car, there are many moving parts to a business. When those parts are set into aligned motion, you gain speed and may cover great distances. However, with a car, as with a business, the destination is ultimately up to you.

Some people have a clear destination in mind when they go for a drive. Others just want to enjoy the experience of driving. A few want to learn more about speed training, and gaining skills and precision, or mastering the racetrack. Cars serve many different goals. Similarly, businesses serve many types of goals—both for the destination and for the process of getting there. But what are these things called goals?

The Anatomy of Effective Goals

Whenever I work with an entrepreneur who seems lost or caught up in petty details, I try to understand the goals that this person is striving to achieve. Usually I find that their goals are either not big enough, or that it is time to change the game and set new goals. With newer, more relevant and more challenging goals in place, all of a sudden the lost entrepreneur is happy and vibrant again.

There are three elements that differentiate effective goals from their ineffective counterparts:

1. **Scope and Meaning**
2. **Risk**
3. **Perspective**

Scope and Meaning

Often, entrepreneurs start picking on inconsequential details and problems if the scope they are working within is too limited. Linked directly with scope is meaning. Meaningful goals and aspirations make a difference to entrepreneurs and impact how they think and operate in the world. Too often, goals are uninspired.

Which of your goals excites you the most?

Risk

The size of your goals is more a function of the nature of risk involved rather than the number of to-do's that need to be accomplished. When risk is present, there is uncertainty present; we are not quite sure if we can do what we set out to accomplish. This can be very exciting—we become exhilarated when we accomplish goals in the face of risk.

Too much risk, by comparison, may be immobilizing—just like a deer caught in the headlights of an oncoming car. Yet an effective challenge that stretches us by pushing at the edges of our comfort zone catches our attention just about every time.

Which of your goals carries an effective balance of risk for you?

Perspective

Effective goals help to shape our perspectives. We spend lots of time on what we look at, but very little time on where we look from. If you want to double (or triple or quadruple) the size of your business within the next two to three years, you cannot afford to get bogged down in basic issues or trivial details. You need to handle these and then move on to the bigger issues that are required to achieve your more substantive goals.

Perspective allows you to put the day-to-day issues in their appropriate context. You are less likely to lose track of the larger issues when you are in the midst of accomplishing larger goals and objectives.

You may want to do a little check of your own. Are your goals substantive in scope and meaning? Is there enough of a risk to keep your attention, but not too much so as to overwhelm you? Do your goals allow you to look from a larger perspective? Now is the time to adjust your goals so that they serve you.

Exercise: Setting Some Initial Goals

1. Please write down your top three goals in each of these important areas of life:

a. Family

_____
_____
_____

b. Social Relationships

_____
_____
_____

c. Personal Growth

_____
_____
_____

d. Financial Security

_____
_____
_____

e. Spiritual

_____
_____
_____

f. Community Involvement

_____
_____
_____

g. Health and Fitness

_____
_____
_____

h. Hobbies (sports, recreation, relaxation, travel, etc.)

_____
_____
_____

i. Contribution to Others

_____
_____
_____

j. Other Areas

_____
_____
_____

2. How, specifically, will you use your business, as it grows, to support you in achieving these personal goals?

_____
_____
_____

3. As your company evolves, what are your goals to grow your skills professionally?

_____
_____
_____

4. What level of growth would be needed in your business for you to reach both your personal and professional goals? Please be specific.

_____

_____

_____

5. What level of growth for your business would really excite you? Double? Triple? Quintuple? A ten-fold increase? Even larger? What excites you about that? (Please note: you will be using the goals you set here to build your organizational structure in chapter 7.)

_____

_____

_____

Why is writing down your goals so important?

A study was done in 1953 at Yale University in which students of the graduating class were interviewed just before they left school. They were asked, among other things, how many of them had a clearly defined set of goals with a written plan of action. Only 3% had a clear, written plan for their lives with a specific set of goals. In 1973, twenty years later, they went back to interview the surviving class members of 1953 and found that the 3% that had written down their goals seemed more happy, more well adjusted and more excited about their lives. The one very measurable thing was that the 3% were worth more financially than the other 97% combined.

6. For the level of increase that you identified in question 5, please answer the following questions. Remember, you are doing this for yourself, so don't hold back – the more clear you are at this stage, the more effective the rest of the growth process becomes.

a. What would this increase do for you personally?

_____
_____
_____

b. What would this increase do for your professional growth? Who would you become in the process of achieving this level of growth?

_____
_____
_____

c. How would this increase impact your personal income? How about your financial net worth?

_____
_____
_____

d. Describe what a typical day in your life would be like when your business is at that level. Please be specific, starting with when you wake up in the morning, and going right until you go to sleep that night. *(use extra paper as needed)*

_____
_____
_____

e. Which activities would you like to be spending your time on at your business?

_____
_____
_____

f. Which activities would you like to delegate to others?

_____
_____
_____

g. How long will it take you to achieve this level of growth in your business?

h. Meaningful goals and aspirations make a difference to entrepreneurs and impact how they think and operate in the world. Too often, goals are uninspired. Which of your goals excite you the most?

Exercise: What Do You REALLY Want?

Now that you've established some preliminary goals for yourself, let's dig a little deeper with this question of what you want to achieve as a result of your business venture. After all, it is you who gets to say how your business goes. The key here is to get clear about how you want the business to serve you in your life. What follows is a number of questions. These questions are designed to get you thinking of some of the different dimensions of how a business might serve your life at a deeper level.

1. On a scale of one to ten, how would you rate the importance of each of these areas: (1 = not important, 10 = very important)

Family	1 2 3 4 5 6 7 8 9 10
Social Relationships	1 2 3 4 5 6 7 8 9 10

Growing your Business	1 2 3 4 5 6 7 8 9 10
Spiritual	1 2 3 4 5 6 7 8 9 10
Community Involvement	1 2 3 4 5 6 7 8 9 10
Avocations/Hobbies	1 2 3 4 5 6 7 8 9 10
Health and Fitness	1 2 3 4 5 6 7 8 9 10
Professional Development	1 2 3 4 5 6 7 8 9 10
Personal Growth	1 2 3 4 5 6 7 8 9 10
Taking Time Off	1 2 3 4 5 6 7 8 9 10

2. If I asked your best friend or partner what is one thing that lights you up when you talk about it, what would he or she say?

_____
_____
_____

3. If you could be doing whatever you wanted (and money was no obstacle), what would it be?

_____
_____
_____

4. What is something that you love to do—something that gives you energy?

5. With whom (i.e. what types of people) do you enjoy working, playing, interacting?

6. What inspires or motivates you?

7. What does financial independence mean to you?

8. When would you like to be financially independent?

9. How much is enough for you to be financially independent? (Please refer to the Financial Independence Calculator)

10. What size of organization do you need to build in order to accomplish your goals for financial independence? Are you willing to build such an organization?

___

11. Is there anything that happened to you at work recently that excited you or gave you energy? Provide an example.

___

12. Is there anything that you did recently that drained your energy? If so, what was it?

___

13. What accomplishments or activities do you take pride in?

___

14. What kind of legacy do you want to leave behind?

___

15. If you knew you couldn't fail, what would you take on?

___

The Financial Independence Calculator

One question that entrepreneurs are often asked (and ask themselves) is, "How much is enough?" This is a very difficult question for many entrepreneurs to answer—usually because the answer keeps changing. While it may not be a static target, at least we have a way to set an initial goal, and to update it over time. Here is a simple formula that may make that question an easier one for you to tackle. By using this formula, you can update your financial goals over time, based upon the new and evolving circumstances you will inevitably encounter over your entrepreneurial career.

The formula follows a three-step process:

Step 1: Calculate the annual return

Annual Return = Principal x Safe Interest Rate

Annual Return: the return you would receive on your investment, without depleting the principal.

Principal: the net, liquid, after-tax proceeds from your business activities. This could be made up of proceeds from the sale of your business, after you paid whatever taxes you would owe on that sale.

Safe Interest Rate: an interest rate that is roughly half of what you would hope and/or expect to get from a large monetary investment. For example, if you think you should reasonably be able to get 10% on your money with professional assistance, then the safe interest rate is 5%.

Step 2: Calculate your Net Annual Spending Money

Annual Return − Taxes = Net Annual Spending Money

Taxes: the income taxes you would owe each year on the interest (or other return) on your investment.

Net Annual Spending Money: what's left after taxes for you to be able to spend each year, without touching the principal.

Step 3: Calculate your Net Monthly Spending Money

Net Annual Spending Money ÷ 12 = Net Monthly Spending Money

Net Monthly Spending Money: what you can spend on a monthly basis without touching the principal.

An Example

What if I wanted $250,000 per year ($20,833 per month after taxes) to live on for the rest of my life?

If I could build my business so that I ended up with $10 million after capital gains taxes, and I assumed a 5% safe interest rate (half of the 10% I really believe I can get), fully taxable at the maximum tax rate (let's say 50% goes to the tax man), the formula would go as follows:

STEP 1:
$10 million x 5% per year = $500,000 per year. This amount would be the annual return before paying taxes.

STEP 2:
$500,000 per year (the return) − $250,000 (the taxes at 50%) = $250,000 per year (the net spending money)

STEP 3:

$250,000 net spending money ÷ 12 = $20,833 per month.

By this example, using the assumptions that we made, if you had $10 million in after-tax assets, generating a 5% cash return that was fully taxable at a 50% tax rate, then you would generate $20,833 per month for the rest of your life, without ever touching the principal. If that is enough for you to be fully financially independent, then you are all set. If you only needed $10,000 per month, you would only need $5 million in principal.

If $20,833 per month is more than you need, then scaling the monthly income back will reduce the amount of principal you need. If $20,833 is not enough, then you can always increase the $10 million to an amount that will give you the net income you desire. If you need $30,000+ per month, you would increase the $10 million to $15 million to achieve this goal.

NET ANNUAL SPENDING MONEY

After-tax monthly income	$20,833.00
x 12 months	$250,000.00
Add taxes (50%)	$250,000.00
Total income (tax in)	$500,000.00
Capital at 5% return	$10,000,000.00

What does your financial independence calculation look like?

After tax monthly income $_____

x 12 months $_____

Add taxes (_____%) $_____

Total income (tax in) $_____

Safe Interest Rate of _____% $_____

Special Note

This does not require that you commit yourself to any particular type of investment. The only condition is that the annual growth must be able to be spent each year. For example, if you invested in real estate, then using rental income as your return would give you cash returns, but to just rely on the asset growth of the property doesn't give you any cash. The equity increase may only be tapped upon sale of the asset, so that doesn't work to give you monthly income. You can't spend half a door at retirement, but this doesn't mean that real estate is a bad investment (nor does it mean that it's a good investment). It just means that you need to look at investments (whether in real estate or something else) that generate a sufficient monthly cash return to meet your goals. Please check with your financial advisor.

The Financial Significance Calculator

Financial independence is a very important goal for most entrepreneurs, but it is not the only financial goal. For many, the opportunity to contribute to others in meaningful ways is just as (if not more) important than financial independence. This leaves us with the following question:

How do you build financial significance into your financial independence goals?
Part of the purpose of using the "safe interest rate" of approximately one half what you would normally expect to generate is to leave some of the return available for your other contributions in life.

In our previous example, we used an interest rate of 5%, which is one half of the 10% you might expect to achieve (if that is your expectation).

Now, if you earned 8% instead of 5%, where would you like to invest – or contribute – the other 3%? In our previous example, an additional 3% would generate an additional $300,000 per year (or $25,000 per month) before tax. Since this is a contribution and not consumption, there is a good chance that these funds will be tax-preferred, or perhaps even fully tax deductible. In what kinds of ways could you make a difference in the world if, in addition to your financial independence, you set yourself up to contribute a significant amount to others?

This strategy aligns your goals for contributions to others or to your community (however large you determine your community to be) with your goals for financial independence.

Try calculating your own numbers on the next page.

Example

Capital	$10,000,000
Interest (3%)	$300,000
Monthly Significance Fund	$25,000

Your Numbers

Capital	$_____
Interest (3%)	$_____
Monthly Significance Fund	$_____

You Don't Need to Wait

If this is your strategy, then even as you grow and develop your business, you can always set aside 3% of your annual earnings toward those contribution or significance goals in the meantime. For many entrepreneurs, this adds the extra juice that makes the whole thing more rewarding and more fun.

With these ideas to support you, you will be better equipped to sort out both your financial and non-financial goals and objectives, so that you may truly set up your business to serve and support your goals and commitments in your life.

CHAPTER 6

Your Profit

Your Profit

There are two issues to consider when determining where the value in your business lies:

1: YOUR PROFIT

Where is the value for you, the business owner? This question will be addressed in this chapter.

2: CUSTOMER VALUE

Where is the value for your customers? This question will be addressed in the next chapter.

Together, your profit and customer value form the Value Exchange. If both you and your customers continue to get value from the exchange, then you will continue to do business. Without a viable value exchange there is no sustainable business.

Your Profit

As you plan growth strategies for your business, one of the critical elements is to determine, in as much detail as possible, the answers to these questions about the current and future profitability of your company.

1. To what extent has the company been profitable up until now?
2. To what levels have the profits occurred to date within each department or division of the company?
3. Is the company structured for a profit? If not, what has to change in order to structure it for a profit?

4. Which customers are the most lucrative (in terms of profit margins, not just sales)?
5. What are the sources of these most lucrative customers?
6. Which product/service lines are most profitable?
7. What will be the impact of a growth plan for each of the product/service lines of the company?
8. Which product/service lines does it make the most sense to expand?
9. Are there products/services that should be reduced or eliminated from the product mix?
10. Which new customers does it make the most sense to seek out?
11. What are the best possible sources of new, profitable customers?
12. Where do the future profits in the company lie?

There will be an opportunity for you to work through these questions at the end of this chapter, but first you need to gather some information that will provide you with a thorough understanding of your company's recent and current financial state.

Most business owners have a general intuitive sense about these things, and many have reviewed some of the details necessary to ascertain the answers to the previous questions.

Yet far too often, the information available comes from an accounting system that was designed for tax and compliance purposes, not for business management purposes. The result is that information received from the accounting program is cumbersome at best, and insufficient (or non-existent) at worst.

If you really want to determine the answers to the questions listed above, then you will need to roll up your sleeves and dig in to your finances. In order to do this, you will need some very specific information about your business.

Essential to effectively identifying the sources of current and future profits within your company is gathering and sorting out the necessary information.

What to Collect

The basic information to collect includes the following:

1. The past three to five years' financial statements (balance sheets and income statements). The information from these extended statements, if organized correctly, will provide lots of information about the trends that have occurred within the company.

2. The last twelve months' income statements on a monthly basis.

3. A current, aged Accounts Receivable listing and an aged Accounts Payable list.

4. A customer list that includes gross sales per customer for the past year and, if available, gross margin. Two or three years' worth of this data is better, as long as you can access the additional information relatively easily.

5. Information on what divisions of the company (and from which salespeople) the customers were gained. What were the products or services that were purchased? From which specific location (or department) were the sales generated?

6. Included in the customer list, identify the original source of that customer (i.e. how did you get that customer lead in the first place?).

By collecting and sorting the information listed above, you will have what you need to gain further insights into the profitability of your company.

Incomplete Information

One of the things you may discover is that some of this information is not readily available from your current systems. Notice what you can readily access and what you cannot. Pull together what you can, and then ask yourself, "What changes to my system would I have to make in order to gain easy access to the missing information?" Then build a plan to make those changes.

By identifying the changes to your information systems necessary to gain useful management information, you will be able to incorporate those adjustments into your systems as they evolve, allowing you access to better information and better business decisions.

Organizing the Information

If you have pulled together all this information, you are probably asking yourself, "What now?"

Begin with your monthly Income Statements. Starting with the first month, put all of the categories noted on the statement down column A of a Microsoft Office Excel spreadsheet. Then , in columns B through M, list each of the months, using column N to total each category. Then input the monthly information into the spreadsheet so that you have one column for each month. This allows for easier analysis of the information when the time comes.

Then take the three to five annual financial statements (both balance sheets and income statements) and do the same thing. Input all the balance sheets into one spreadsheet and the income statements into another. Again, this will allow for the trends and shifts over that period to be identified.

As for the customer lists, set these aside for now. We will come back to them later.

A Good Accountant

There are a number of things to look for on your financial statements. Rather than turn this into a lesson on how to read financials, I am simply going to list some of the things that I look at. If you have difficulty with any of this, please meet with your accountant or financial advisor to work through this information with you.

If you don't have an accountant, go get a good one, quick. Even if you don't have a lot of money at the moment, if you plan on earning lots, a good accountant will serve you well. How do you find a good one? Ask others whose opinions you respect for a few referrals to good accountants, and then go interview a couple of them. Find someone in whom you have confidence, and whom you understand and feel good about.

Get potential accountants to explain things to you, and if you still don't understand, keep looking. Remember: they are there to help you, and if you don't understand what they are saying, they are making things more complicated than necessary. A really good accountant will match his or her level of expertise with your level of expectation. You don't need to become an expert to work with a good accountant. They already are the experts. Their job includes explaining things so you understand your own money.

What to Look For

The purpose of analyzing your financial statements is to gain a clear picture of exactly what the landscape looks like in your business at the moment. You may have done well in the past, but what are things like today? What might you expect moving into the future? What are the trends that you want to either capitalize upon or to avoid?

The questions on the next few pages will help you to gain the clarity you will need to grow.

The Income Statements

(also known as Profit & Loss, or P&L, Statements)

1. Is your company making any money? To determine this, check the Net Income line of the Income Statements.

2. How much money is your company making? Is this before or after your wages? If your wages have already been listed as part of the company's expenses, then you may want to add them back to confirm how much money you are really earning.

3. What percentage of your gross sales represents your net income plus your wages? Is it a healthy percentage?

4. What has been the trend with the sales levels? If there have been large shifts over the past months (or last few years), what accounted for those changes? Was each a permanent change, or a temporary one?

5. How stable is your Gross Profit as a percentage of your sales? Is that growing or shrinking? What is the cause of changes in gross profit that may have occurred? Will those changes likely stay, or were they temporary (e.g. you may have gained a special discount for your inventory on a one-time basis only, or incurred a one-time expense to try a new product line)?

6. How much gross profit do you need to generate each month to cover your fixed monthly expenses? What is your break-even level of sales? Has it shifted over the past few years? What has caused those shifts? Are these factors likely to continue?

7. Do your monthly fixed expenses seem right? Are there any anomalies that stick out when you look at your monthly numbers over the past year? If so, what accounted for these changes?

8. Is there enough cash coming in to pay the bills on a regular basis?

9. Is your company on an upward trend or a downward trend? In gross sales? In gross profits? In net income? In capturing market share? For each major product/service line? Overall, how well is your company doing in terms of generating the money you want?

10. Is your company structured for an adequate profit, both in terms of percentages and in dollars, at its current size? Will that likely need to change as the company grows? What to check for here is what additional expenses will need to be incurred in order to have a significant increase in sales. If your margins are incredibly thin, then you may need to grow your company a lot just to reach your target net income. What will be the risks of doing this? Are the risks worth it?

If everything has to go perfectly for you to achieve your financial goals, you may want to rethink the game. This is a very good conversation to have with your accountant or other advisors. I review these types of issues with clients all the time.

The Balance Sheet

(also known as the Statement of Assets & Liabilities)

1. How solvent is your company? How much of a financial reserve is there? Is it growing or shrinking?

2. How current are your Accounts Receivable? Are there any problems evident from this document? (Check your aged Receivables.)

3. How up to date are your Accounts Payable? Is your company keeping current with all the expenditures you are incurring on a regular basis?

4. What is your Current Ratio (Current Assets divided by Current Liabilities)? Is it larger than 1? If so, that means that you have enough money in the bank, plus your accounts receivables and other liquid assets, to cover your short-term liabilities. If it is less than 1, you may be short of cash. Either way, you want to be clear on just what kind of financial shape you are currently in.

5. What are listed as your long-term Liabilities (long-term debts of the company)? Is this growing or shrinking? For what purpose was the debt in this section of the Balance Sheet originally acquired? How was the money used? Is the debt putting a squeeze on the cash flow of the company, or is it easy to cover? How quickly is this debt going down? At what interest rate is your debt being carried? High? Low? Is there room to renegotiate the interest rate?

6. Is the Net Equity (Retained Earnings + Net Income) a positive or negative number? In other words, do you have more assets than liabilities, or do you have more liabilities than assets? While it is not uncommon for a small company to owe more than it owns, this is not the desired state. You will want to change this over time.

Special Note

There are a whole host of questions and issues that your financial statements will reveal to you (or to your accountant, your business consultant or financial advisor, who can help you with this). These are too numerous to cover completely here. The point of these questions is to get you started at looking at the details of your current money situation. In growing your business, you will want to have a positive influence on your financial situation, regardless of your current position. Get clear on the starting point so that you can measure the changes as they occur.

Some people avoid looking at their numbers because the numbers don't look very good. I see this all the time. Growing a business, however, requires that you face the truth, and sometimes the truth isn't pretty. Don't let your numbers get you down, no matter what they look like. Anyone can make judgments about someone else's money. The point of this exercise is not to make you feel bad that your numbers aren't stronger than they currently are. Rather, the point is merely to get you to identify the starting line for your future growth.

One of the first keys to improving any situation is to tell the truth about what is there, but just as important as not overstating that is not understating the way things are either. Tell it like it is, but don't exaggerate (either positively or negatively). I have seen people beat themselves up over their money situation, claiming that it is worse than it is. That is not useful at all. That just makes you feel bad and will likely get (or keep) you stuck.

However, don't tell yourself that things are better than they really are, either. I have seen people who delude themselves and avoid the reality of difficult financial circumstances, which only makes matters worse. Rather than address a difficult situation directly, they avoid it, only to leave things too long and risk losing the business entirely when they could have taken corrective action and made things better.

Let's move on to your customer list.

The Customer List

To organize the customer list so that the information will be useful, I recommend that you import the information into an Excel chart with the following titles, for easy sorting.

Cust. Name	Date Started	Original Source	Product(s)/ Service(s)	Annual Gross Sales	Annual Gross Profit

You may be able to get this information from your accounting software and import it directly, at least for the gross sales levels. Then, you may have to add the information about when customers started buying from you, how you got them as a lead, what products/services they bought from you, and what the gross profit level has been from them as customers.

In many instances I find that clients don't have the Gross Profit per customer available. That is ok for now. Just start asking your bookkeeper or accountant how you will be able to change your data collection moving forward so that you start to track this information. Remember, what you make is nice, but it is what you keep that counts! So, gross profit per client is extremely important, especially if you grow fairly quickly. It is not always the biggest customers who contribute the most to your profitability. This type of analysis is very useful for clarifying exactly where your profits are coming from.

Sorting

Once the data is in Excel (whether by direct import, or whether you have a clerk type the information in directly), you can start sorting it. The first way to sort this data is by Gross Sales per customer. You want to see how your customers stack up against one another. From whom have the bulk of your sales been coming up until now?

Now, some people, when they see the request for this type of information, will respond with, "I already know who my biggest customers are. I don't need to do this part." Well, if I was only looking for who your biggest customers are, I would probably agree with you. However, I want you to look for much more than that. If you have Gross Profit (GP) per customer, then do a second sort, to rank that from highest to lowest. See if there are any shifts that occur in the data. Are your biggest customers the most lucrative, or have they moved down the list? Any surprises showing up here?

Quintiles

The next analysis to conduct is to break your customer list up into quintiles, ranked from highest to lowest sales. You do this two ways. The first way is to take your total sales volume and divide it by five. For example, let's say that you have gross sales of $2 million. Then each quintile will be $400,000. Add up your customer sales, starting from the top and working your way down, until you reach $400,000. Draw a line below that point. This group of people represents your top quintile of customers. Then count up the next $400,000 and do the same again (and again and again and again) until you have your customer list broken up into five groups representing approximately $400,000 each. Then count how many customers are in each quintile. The next question to ask yourself is, How much money and effort goes into serving each quintile? This type of analysis allows you to gain further clarification on where your most profitable customers are—or, said a different way, what is your "sweet spot".

By the way, it is not always the biggest customers who form a company's sweet spot. If it is really easy to serve a mid-level customer, but takes a great toll on your company to deliver the services necessary to keep the big ones, you may find that it is more lucrative to expand in that mid zone rather than at the top.

Remember, we are not talking about what customers to cut (though you may want to do that too, especially if your lowest-quintile customers are taking too much of your time without an offsetting benefit), but rather what customers and markets to expand to increase your profits as you grow.

The second way to break your customer list into quintiles (again, ranked by sales, from highest to lowest) is to take the total number of customers and divide that by five, and mark off the quintiles. For example, if you have 165 customers, then each quintile will be 33 customers big. Counting from the top, separate each customer group and then add up the revenues (and GP if you have that) for each of the five quintiles. Again, you will see where your sales and profits come from. How much in sales and profit does each of these quintiles provide? Very revealing stuff!

Other Sorts

The next sort to do is still a ranked sort (from highest sales/GP to lowest)—this time by product/service type provided. Which product lines are getting you the most sales/profits? Which of them are less lucrative? How are the sales dispersed through your product/service lines?

Then do a sort by source of lead. Which lead sources have helped you grow the most? Which ones have not improved your situation? Customers from which lead sources have been with you the longest? Is there a difference in customer longevity based upon the source of lead?

When we did this with our own company, we found that almost everyone who worked with us came as referrals from other happy clients (not a surprise to us). What did surprise me was that of the few people who came to us from a directory listing (that is, from the yellow pages when we first started out over fifteen years ago), none of them stayed with us for long. Yet with those who came to us from referrals, the average time of working together was much longer.

Upon further examination, we found that those who were referred to us were prepared for the time and energy it takes to properly grow a business on a sustainable basis. The others came looking for a magic bullet of some sort. We quickly changed our approach, pushing people away if they didn't come to us by referral until they had talked with people who had dealt with us before. This changed our ratios and allowed us to work more effectively with people's expectations, and deliver strong client results, regardless of the source of the lead.

If the source of the leads is different salespeople, you will be able to see, first-hand, the effectiveness of each of your sales staff. If you have different offices, then you can see the sales by department, by office or by geographic region. Then, within each of these areas, you will be able to further break down your customer lists to see more specific trends. Then by comparing the sales, in particular by product/service line across geographic zones, you will have access to even more trends.

These are the analyses that larger companies conduct routinely to assist them in managing their overall operations and targets for growth. They work just as well for small companies. All you have to do is pull the data together and view it in these alternate ways, looking for the trends as you go.

The Point of This Analysis

After looking through and analyzing your information, start to determine where your highest and most easily achieved levels of future profit lie. This is commonly referred to as the low-hanging fruit. If you can pick the low-hanging fruit first, it will help you to fund your growth along the way, rather than needing to run out and borrow a bunch of money to expand. Increasing sales is generally the best way to pay for your growth. You don't have to pay that back to anyone, be it a lender or an investor.

Not only do you want to clarify where the low-hanging fruit is, you also want to identify what your sales/product/customer composition will be as you double, (or triple, or quadruple, etc.) your business. The clearer you are on your product mix and your customer mix as you expand, the easier it will be to grow.

Take the time to work through your numbers and to determine where to grow. Even if you already know most of this, the previous exercises will give you direct access to more aspects of the terrain you will have to cover, as you grow your business, consistent with your goals and commitments in life.

Exercise: Your Profit

As you plan your growth strategies, one of the critical elements is to determine, in as much detail as possible, the answers to the following series of questions about the current and future profitability of your company. Answering these questions will help you clarify the results of your analyses.

1. To what extent has your company been profitable up until now? What trends have you noticed?

2. Is your company structured for profit? If not, what has to change in order to structure it for profit?

3. Which product/service lines were most profitable?

4. What will be the impact of a growth plan for each of the product/service lines of the company?

5. Which product/service lines does it make the most sense to expand? Are there products or services that should be reduced or eliminated from the mix?

6. Where do the future profits of the company lie?

7. What will be the next three actions you will take to increase your profits?

_____

_____

_____

Numbers come to life when you understand that achieving your dreams lives in the numbers. The task is to understand the relationship between the numbers and your goals and commitments.

If you don't have a profound relationship with the numbers, whether you are a salesperson just starting out or a business owner, you are lost. The numbers are important because they provide an accurate story of how you are being paid for delivering value, interacting with customers, etc.

Go through everything—line by line, item by item.

Special Note

Rather than borrowing money or using your own to grow your business, you can use your profitability (as you grow) to help you continue to grow. If you can identify who the most profitable customers are, and you go after more of them first, you can fund your growth using this mechanism. Ask yourself, How can I fund my growth internally? Look at your financial statements and identify where you are making money, where there is leakage and where there is excess capacity, and restructure accordingly.

Exercise: Customer Profitability

Once you have prepared a spreadsheet on your own customers, think about how you might acquire more top customers—either by referrals, or from your current large customers, or by building your relationship with those customers who are in the second or third quintiles. Try to determine the following things as you examine your second and third quintiles:

1. What percentage of each customer's business are you already getting?
_____
_____
_____

2. How lucrative is that business?
_____
_____
_____

3. What are the chances of getting referrals from those customers?
_____
_____
_____

4. Which customer groups were the most lucrative (in terms of profit margins, not just sales)? If you can't tell, how do you need to change your accounting systems to track gross profit per customer in the future?
_____
_____
_____

5. What will be the impact of creating a growth plan for each of the various customer groups you have identified?
_____
_____
_____

Now, look at your lowest tiers of customers and see if they are giving you one-off business or whether there is potential to grow them into repeat customers. Alternatively, if they are not profitable to you on an on-going basis or if there is no potential for growth, you might consider leaving them behind. You may refer them to another service provider, which will free you to go after the customers in your sweet spot.

Special Note

When you have a business with high variable costs, you tend to protect your profit margin. Another important thing to consider is this: if you have a business with high variable costs, you'll be less likely to drop your prices; if you have a company with low variable costs and high fixed costs, it is more likely that you will 1) drop your prices and 2) be susceptible to price competition. There tends to be more price competition when there are high fixed costs and fewer variable costs.

An example of a business with low variable costs is an airline company. It doesn't matter if planes are full or half full, the costs for fuel, the amortization costs for the airplane, etc. will remain more or less fixed for each flight.

Just by listing the information in this way, trends begin to emerge and it makes it much easier to strategize a game plan for growth.

Collecting Information: Follow-Up

One of the things you may discover is that some of this information is not readily available from your current systems. Notice what you can readily access and what you cannot. Pull together what you can and ask yourself, What changes to the system would I have to make in order to gain easy access to the missing information?

By identifying the changes to your information systems necessary to gain useful management information, you will be able to incorporate those adjustments into your systems as they evolve, allowing you access to better information and better business decisions.

By collecting and sorting the information listed above, you will have what you need to gain insights into the profitability of your company as you seek to gain and keep more customers at a profit, growing your business in a way that is consistent with your goals and commitments in life.

CHAPTER 7

Customer Value

Customer Value

Customer Value is the other half of the Value Exchange. Your profit will only be sustained if your customers continue to gain value from their interactions with you, and keep spending money on your goods and services as you grow.

In this chapter we will be examining:

- How you clarify your value proposition for your most profitable customers
- How to clarify and expand your unique factors
- How to develop your Unique Process and how to label it
- What is your *desired* customer experience of value
- What is the *actual* experience of value that your current customers gain (using customer satisfaction surveys)
- The development/enhancement of your marketing materials to communicate the customer value in a manner that will attract more of the best customers to you

Your Value Proposition

What is it that your customers value about the product or service you offer? What makes you different from your competition? This is why they buy from you, instead of your competitor. Just what makes your company so special? If your answer is "nothing", then you may have a difficult time growing, except as the lowest-priced alternative. What would your customers say about this? When was the last time that you asked them?

I know these are a lot of questions to ask all at once. However, this is one of the most important areas there is to cover when seeking large-scale growth (or growth of any kind). If you are clear on what your customers value about you and your company, then you can grow. If not, the job will be very difficult.

Who are your desired customers? Did the last series of exercises, where you examined your current customer base, assist you in clarifying this for yourself? If so, then great. But what if your company is too new to have a bunch of customers to assist you in gaining that level of clarity? Or what if the customer list from your current or past operations is not consistent with the new customers you intend to target as part of your growth plan? How do you clarify this for yourself?

The Credo

At Kaizen Consulting, we have a tool that we call the Credo. The Credo is a tool to help you to think through and describe your company, your products and services, your desired customers and the benefits of your offerings in a direct, straight-forward manner. Often built as a one-page document, this is a simple form of introduction that may be sent in advance of a meeting with a potential customer or provided as part of a "leave behind" package or brochure to reinforce discussions in a meeting.

It has been said that the Credo is the window to the soul of your business. It allows people to see right into the core of your company in a very simple manner. In addition to helping others gain clarity regarding your business, it also helps you to speak to the core clearly, for yourself.

There are four parts to the Credo. They are:

1. Who am I?
2. What do I do?
3. Who are my customers?
4. How do they benefit (from their perspective)?

That's it. Sounds simple enough, doesn't it? Yet it is trickier than it first appears. We have had people who are starting out in business struggle with this little tool for all four months of *The Business Builder*™, one of our programs. We have had multi-millionaires with twenty-plus years experience in their businesses who struggle with this little tool for... you guessed it... four months. Though it seems easy enough, it pierces to the core. That is part of what makes it so useful as a tool, and so difficult to crystalize.

By building your Credo, you gain access to a whole new level of clarity on what you do, for whom you do it and how people win by what you provide to them. With that increased clarity, it is easier to describe to others, too.

Let's take a more detailed look at the components of this simple yet powerful tool.

1. WHO AM I?

This question seems easy enough, and it is. Here, you merely want to clarify your own name, your company name, your profession (if applicable) and perhaps the geographic span of your operations. So far, so good.

2. WHAT DO I DO?

What is your product/service offering? Here is where the first twist occurs. Instead of stating this from your perspective, you want to state it from your customer's perspective. An accountant, for instance, might say that she is an accountant, or that she provides accounting services. These two comments are made from the perspective of the accountant, not the customer's perspective. By the way, if she says that she is an accountant, that is who she is, not what she does.

To say it from the customer's perspective, you will need to answer a bit of a different question. That question is, "What is the result you assist your customer to generate?" To state what you do, from the perspective of the result you assist people to generate for themselves is taking on the customer's perspective.

Back to our accountant: The answer to this customer-focused question might be, "I assist clients to minimize their taxes, and meet their tax-filing responsibilities." The first response, providing accounting services, is very close to the second one, assisting clients to minimize their taxes and meet their tax filing responsibilities. However, the thing that has changed is the focus. Instead of telling you what I do from *my* perspective, I am now telling you what I do from *your* perspective (if I were an accountant, anyway). That difference may seem subtle, but it is far reaching.

3. WHO ARE MY CUSTOMERS?

In this segment, rather than trying to cover everyone who has the potential to be a customer, the key is to identify your ideal or best possible customer. If you are growing, that is who you want to attract to your business. There may be others whom you will serve, yet identifying the best customers for you makes it easier to find them, and to serve them. So instead of a wide, inclusive field of vision, you want to develop a laser eye for who, specifically, you would like to work with as your customers.

4. HOW DO THEY BENEFIT (FROM THEIR PERSPECTIVE)?

People buy for their own reasons, not yours. What is the win for them, from their perspective? This is where people get mixed up between features, results and benefits.

- Feature: lightning-fast air bags in your car
- Result: the bags catch you before you head through the windshield
- Benefit: driving with peace of mind

The benefit speaks to the impact on your customer of having achieved the desired result.

Notice that driving with peace of mind is all about the driver's win, not any particular details of the car, or its safety features. That is what you want to identify for your product or service offering. As a result of working with you, how will your customers win, from their perspective? Another way to consider this is to ask yourself: What is the impact of my customer achieving the result I assist them to achieve?

The Credo is a solid start in clarifying your value proposition. The key to using this tool to state your customer's value is that the Credo sets it up from your customer's perspective, not yours. What you do is stated as the result you assist your customer to generate, and the benefit statement is clearly about them, not you.

What if you are not sure how you really create and provide measurable value for your customers? Then you may want to use the following tool to assist you to clarify and brainstorm this for yourself.

Exercise: What is Your Credo?

1. Who am I? (Your identity)	3. Who are my customers? (Identify your ideal customer)
2. What do I do? (Results you help them generate)	4. How do they benefit? (Their win —the impact of the result—from their perspective)

Generating Commerce: Creating Value

In life, there are only three ways to make money. You can either:

1. print it yourself, (with your own printing press in the basement?)
2. steal it, or
3. talk someone else out of theirs.

Unless you are willing to risk spending a good deal of time behind bars, number three is probably the only viable alternative listed above.

Now you may be wondering, What if I win the lottery? or What if I gain an inheritance? These scenarios both qualify under the third method. In the case of an inheritance, you obviously talked nicely enough (or no worse than your siblings or other relatives) to be included in the will. In the case of the lottery, you are making a deal with someone that if this particular set of numbers gets drawn, then they pay you lots. If that isn't talking people out of their money, I don't know what is!

I asked a group recently about the quantity and frequency of money they wanted to generate. The unanimous decision was, "Lots, often." The only way you will be able to talk someone out of their money on a frequent basis is to make it a better deal for them to give you their money than it would be to keep it for themselves. This, we call commerce.

How do you make it a good deal for people and companies to give you their dollars? You create value for them, that's how. The more measurable the value you generate for your customers, the more interested they will be to continue to give you their money. We call this the Value Exchange, and it is the basis of all business.

Specifically, their value gets created as you assist them (with your products and services) to achieve their desired results.

Your Process for Generating Customer Results

People want results in their lives. They buy goods and services in order to achieve results. Your Process is the link between what you offer and how they achieve the results they seek. Where the Credo contains an allegation that people win, your Process becomes the explanation of how they will gain the benefits that you allege in your Credo.

By identifying your process, you are building the bridge for your customers, enabling them to gain confidence that your products and services will give them what they want. This bridge may be used to step your customers through your methodology of product or service delivery, ensuring the desired results.

Elements of an Effective Process

Fundamentally, there are at least three key areas within most effective processes. They are:

1. **Information gathering**
2. **Evaluation and solutions/options development**
3. **Implementation of solution(s)/option(s) to generate the result**

1. INFORMATION GATHERING – THE DIAGNOSTIC SEGMENT

In order to support a customer to generate a result, you will want to understand all you can about that customer. This may include some or all of the segments below:

- Current situation: overview
- Detailed elements of the situation as they apply to you (and your product mix)
- Goals and objectives: either short-, medium- and long-term, or perhaps for the company, as well as the owners or others within an organization or department
- Concerns about obstacles that might impede the attainment of the desired objectives
- Current strategies: what has been done to date to address the concerns
- Priorities: looking from today forward
- Financial considerations: this could be anything from budget to an overall review of the financial scope and/or implications of a project or objective in mind

- Timing: both for your work with the customer overall, and also of each of the top priorities

The more information you are able to gather from your customer, the more effective your solutions will be and the more you will be able to change the basis of comparison from price to other more pertinent factors, like "fit to need".

2. EVALUATION AND SOLUTIONS/OPTIONS DEVELOPMENT

In this segment of the Process, you identify the specific issues that need to be addressed, given the different elements and considerations related to your product and/or service offerings to your customers.

The diagnostic segment might be quite similar among companies with completely varied products and services. This is summarized by questions pertaining to where you are now, where you want to go, what's stopping you and what are your priorities, budget and timing.

The analysis of critical issues and development of solutions need to be customized to the industry and business you are in. These vary dramatically between differing companies and need to be developed based upon the actual procedures you use in support of the development of your customers' desired results.

Examples

A financial planning firm might use the following to describe this segment 2 portion of the process.

Develop strategies and tactics in each of the following (6) areas:
- Money management
- Tax planning
- Retirement planning
- Investment planning

- Estate planning
- Risk management

A public speaking coach, by contrast, might list completely different points as part of segment 2.

Develop strategies in each of the following areas:
- Message development
- Pace
- Connection with the audience
- Use of relevant stories
- Building the major points
- Power of the conclusion
- Call to action
- Post-presentation follow-up

In the next section you will see two different examples of the Process, one from our own business consulting firm and the second from a high-end kitchen cabinet dealer.

In each case, while the first segments are similar to each other, the second segments are completely customized based upon the service offerings involved.

For your Process, you will want to customize this second segment as well.

3. IMPLEMENTATION OF SOLUTIONS/OPTIONS TO GENERATE THE RESULT

Often the implementation portion is pretty straightforward. In this section, you may wish to further demonstrate how you are not just another competitor in your area, but, rather, a unique force in the marketplace.

You may list what might be accomplished in the short-term, the medium-term and the long-term in your business relationship with your customer. As an alternative, you may wish to customize this segment further. Look and see what your process for working with your customers is, and then your job of describing it will be simplified.

The following pages feature two sample processes that are designed to generate results for customers. They are called *The Clarity Process*™ and *The Counterpoint Process*™.

Example One: The Clarity Process™

OBJECTIVES:

- To help you, as you grow your company, to qualify and quantify the size and scope of your opportunities
- To identify the specifics of a strategic implementation plan
- To capture opportunities for growth

INTENDED RESULTS:

You will gain a specific, implementable plan of action to grow your company consistent with your goals and commitments.

THE PROCESS:

Discovery Interview
- Current Status
- Goals and Objectives
- Concerns
- Current Strategies
- Priorities
- Timing

Critical Issues Analysis
- Your Profit
- Customer Value
- Organizational Structure
- Delivery Capacity
- Your People
- New Sales
- Repeat/Referral Business
- Cash Flow
- Alignment of Goals

Strategic Implementation
- Sales
- People
- Structures

Example Two: The Counterpoint Process
INFORMATION
Analysis of current kitchen for function, ergonomics and storage

Listening to your needs:
- Physical parameters
- Cooking style
- Storage and shopping patterns
- Personal priorities and lifestyle
- Budget requirements

Listening to your dreams:
- Collection of ideas for your kitchen
- Kitchens you've had in the past
- Liaison with your designer and architect

Site evaluation:
- Electrical and plumbing
- Construction
- Light and views

The FUNK Chart:
- A navigational tool that eliminates stress and worry

PLANNING

Development of a kitchen concept plan

Analysis and selection:
- Cabinets
- Appliances
- Countertops and finishes
- Plans, evaluations and perspectives
- Needs and desires check
- Drawings and specifications for contractor, electrician and plumber

IMPLEMENTATION

Cabinet material takeoff and listing
- Triple-check: designer, order processor, factory and designer
- Liaison with designers, architects, contractors and others
- Pre-installation meeting:
  - Double check site measurements, electrical and plumbing
- Installation
- Final inspection and touch-up

FOLLOW-UP

- Feature kitchen program
- Six-month and yearly checkup
- Enrollment in Kitchens That Cook

Your Unique Process

What makes your business unique? Whether you have a one-of-a-kind product to sell, or you and your competitors market the same stuff to a similar customer group, there is one thing that differentiates your business from anybody else's business. That differentiator is *you*.

So what, you say? Every individual is unique. We all have different thinking patterns and slightly (or not so slightly) different ways of doing things. That's what makes us different.

How does this translate to your business? Even if you provide the same service as a direct competitor, how you provide that service will be unique to you. What there is to do is to identify the process that you use, put a fancy label on it and you can point to your uniqueness as part of your marketing initiatives.

Let me give you an example. If you ask an academic the difference between twenty post-graduate business courses and an MBA program, most will tell you that it's the label. The difference between taking a bunch of courses, and taking courses within a specific syllabus is that within the MBA program, the courses are chosen to provide a specific type of education rather than a random educational experience.

People like Packaged Stuff...

Whether people are buying a meal at McDonald's or buying high-end engineering services, they tend to prefer to go with bundles and integrated systems. With McDonald's it may be The Happy Meal. With high-end engineering services it could be The Electricity Forum™. In financial planning, it could be The Wealth Creator™. In business consulting, it might be The Profit Navigator™ or The Business Builder™. Labeled processes are more interesting to buyers, as they indicate that the seller has a system that (presumably) is designed to generate a predictable result.

Exercise: What's Your Process?

In the following pages, list the steps that you follow to generate specific results within your business. Once these are listed, think through this process as you have used it with a number of customers. Does your process work consistently? What are the elements of your process that are unique to your organization? What are the benefits that your customers gain as a result of your use of that process on their behalf? By addressing these questions, you will have the basis for developing your unique process and the raw materials for labeling it as well.

Your Process:

_____

_____

The results that your process helps people achieve:

_____

_____

The Steps of Your Process:

1. _____

_____

2. _____

_____

3. _____

_____

4. _____

_____

5. _____

_____

6. _____

7. _____

8. _____

9. _____

10. _____

The Benefits of Your Process:

1. _____

2. _____

3. _____

4. _____

5. _____

6. _____

7. _____

8. _____
_____

9. _____
_____

10. _____
_____

Naming Your Process

When naming your process, you want to include the benefits in the name. As an example, notice that with one of our trademarked programs, The Business Builder™, the name itself states the benefit. People will be able to build their businesses with the assistance of this program. You may also notice that the word "The" has been added to all the labels listed above. That is because each process is unique. Notice it doesn't say "one of many" or "one of a few". It is "The", as in "The One and Only."

This is how much of the intellectual capital in the world is developed. People identify their systems and then they label them with an appropriate label that accurately represents the results that are achieved by using the process in question.

By clarifying your processes and taking the time to label them, you will increase the confidence of your customers in your ability to deliver consistent results, and distinguish your uniqueness in the market.

Safety Tip

You may want to keep your Process to one page and in point form so that you are not divulging all your trade secrets to your competition.

You can always elaborate through a verbal conversation, anchoring added information to some of the key words in your written process, but that added information will not be passed on to your competitors without great effort from your potential customers. This protects (at least somewhat) your strategic advantage, while making the information available to your customers as needed and useful to them.

By demonstrating the level of thoroughness you bring to your Process, you will be better positioned to assist your customers to attain their desired results, and grow your business consistent with your goals and commitments.

The Customer Experience

One of the most difficult tasks as you take on large-scale growth is to maintain or enhance the customer experience of value as you grow. Most small business owners are directly involved in generating that customer experience based on their own personal efforts. In order to grow your business effectively, you will need to generate that experience of value without your direct contact with customers.

Just think about this: How well can your business generate that feeling that stays with your customers—about how well they were served—when it becomes five to ten times its current size? If your personal follow-up call is part of that service, then you will definitely need to replace your own efforts in the customer value experience loop, or you will be the bottle-neck that stops your company from achieving the goals for growth that you seek.

One of the biggest threats when you grow is how to ensure that the customers still gain a solid experience of value even if you are no longer a direct part of the equation.

Quantifying the Customer Experience

A fact that plagues most business owners is that the customer experience of value is usually qualitative, based upon your intuitive sense of what the customer needs, and then proving that. This is very difficult to replicate. As a result, in order to grow you will need to quantify exactly what experience you want your customers to have as they deal with your organization.

There are two levels of the customer experience. The first level is the achievement of the results you promise to deliver. Did the customer get what you promised? If you are an architectural firm, did the customer get the building design, the working drawings and your (or your team's) supervision through a successful construction process? These are the hard deliverables that you promised. These are somewhat easy to measure, though you want to make sure you have mechanisms in place to confirm what you want to promise and for what price, and then how well you deliver what you promise in exchange for your fee.

The second level is far more difficult to measure than the first, but it is just as important to your customer's experience of the value they receive from you. That is their personal experience along the way. This will be measured through their five senses: How do they feel as they go through the process with you? What is their actual experience as you work through your product or service delivery? What would you like that experience to be?

The following questions are designed to assist you to clarify for yourself what is the customer experience of value that you desire to be able to generate for your customers.

List the products and services that you currently provide to your customers. For each product or service, what are the hard deliverables that you want to be able to provide to your customers, both now and as you grow?

Product/Service A: _____

Hard Deliverables:

_____
_____
_____
_____
_____
_____
_____
_____

Product/Service B: _____

Hard Deliverables:

_____
_____
_____
_____
_____
_____
_____
_____

Product/Service C: _____

Hard Deliverables:

_____
_____
_____
_____
_____
_____
_____
_____

Continue this on a separate sheet of paper until you have all of your main products and services covered. Then for each product and each service, what is it that you want your customer to experience along the way?

Now, write out how you see the relationship evolving, and what your customer will experience with each of your main products and services.

Relationship/Experience for A:

_____
_____
_____
_____
_____
_____
_____
_____

Relationship/Experience for B:

_____
_____
_____
_____
_____
_____
_____
_____

Relationship/Experience for C:

_____
_____
_____
_____
_____
_____
_____
_____

Actual Customer Experience

It is nice to desire good things for your customers. The question is, How well are you doing so far? Many people would like to treat the customer even better than they currently do. How close to your desired level of customer care are you operating?

One of the easiest ways to measure customer satisfaction is to go and ask your customers themselves. For years, we have used a series of customer satisfaction surveys to check in with customers of many of our clients, to help the clients determine to what extent they are meeting the expectations of their customers.

Back in the early 1990s there were many organizations and people following the Total Quality Management (TQM) movement in business. They had various versions of customer surveys that companies could use to check their progress with their constituents.

We have an example of such surveys on the next page of this section. By asking your customers how well you are doing, you will gain valuable feedback that will allow you to fine-tune your offering to your customers and to ensure that you can quantify the customer experience of value in preparation for, and throughout the growth of your business.

Surveys provide very useful first-hand information about what is working in your business and what needs work. Keep in mind that every person in your organization needs to be actively engaged in one or both of two specific activities in the company.

They either need to be 1) maintaining or enhancing the customer experience of value, or 2) they need to be protecting and growing your profit. If they are not involved in activities that do one of these two important things, they have no place in your company.

The sample survey that follows is a simple telephone survey that can be conducted with a sampling of anywhere from fifteen to twenty customers. In some cases, we conducted this with fifteen to twenty customers per salesperson (in sales-based organizations) or per practitioner (in the health care professions). These numbers are statistically significant and will yield effective feedback.

By utilizing customer satisfaction surveys, you will be able to check, and then ensure, that you are delivering the customer experience of value that you desire as you grow.

Example: Customer Satisfaction Survey (circle one)

1. Are we available and ready when you require our products or services?
   Superior   Good   Average   Poor

2. Are our staff interested and happy to serve you?
   Superior   Good   Average   Poor

3. Are we dependable, consistent and accurate?
   Superior   Good   Average   Poor

4. Are we trustworthy, reputable and respectable?
   Superior   Good   Average   Poor

5. Are we knowledgeable, informed and competent?
   Superior   Good   Average   Poor

6. Are we confidential and private?
   Superior   Good   Average   Poor

7. Do we willingly explain our products and services to you?
   Superior   Good   Average   Poor

8. Are we friendly, personable and attentive?
   Superior   Good   Average   Poor

9. Are our people courteous and professional?
   Superior   Good   Average   Poor

10. Does the quality of our products and services meet your expectations?
    Superior   Good   Average   Poor

11. Has the work we've done resulted in an improved outcome?
    Superior   Good   Average   Poor

12. Are we worth the expenditure of time and money?
    Superior   Good   Average   Poor

13. Would you use us again?
    Yes   No

14. Would you recommend us to others?
    Yes   No

15. Do you have any suggestions to improve our level of customer service?

Developing Your Marketing Materials

You always need a relationship sufficient to do business. The larger the level of business, the stronger the relationship needs to be. The purpose of marketing materials is to support or enhance the development of relationships with potential customers.

From this perspective, there are five components to effective marketing materials (in terms of relationship development).

These are:
1. **Your Credo**
2. **Your Process**
3. **Credentials**
4. **Testimonials**
5. **Other pertinent material**

1. Your Credo

The first document is the Credo (we reviewed this earlier. Once you have thought through your Credo, you will want to generate a one-page summary, listing the four elements, namely:

1. Who am I
2. What do I do
3. Who are my customers
4. How do they benefit (from their perspective)

By addressing these four elements, you will be able to introduce yourself quite effectively, yet succinctly to new potential customers.

Notice that in point four of the Credo, you make an allegation, alleging that your customers benefit in some meaningful way. This leads to the second component of marketing materials, namely, your Process.

2. Your Process

Where your Credo provides an allegation, your Process (see page 133) provides the explanation. This document provides an overview of the "how". How do you accomplish the results that you support people in attaining? By the end of walking through the Process, your potential customers are left thinking (or saying), "I don't know if they really can do what they are claiming, but if they address these items here in their Process, I can clearly see that I will get the result that they say."

3. Credentials

This is the beginning of the third phase of your marketing materials. Where the Credo makes an allegation, and the Process provides an explanation, the Credentials, Testimonials and Other Pertinent Materials provide the demonstration, or the proof.

What are the backgrounds of your people? What experiences have you gained that are uniquely yours, and which qualify you to assert that your Process works? These demonstrate your ability to get results. Properly addressed, the credentials portion of your marketing materials can give your potential customers increased confidence in your company and in you.

4. Testimonials

Then, with testimonials: What do others have to say about your effectiveness in generating the desired results? The best testimonials tend to come to you unsolicited. However, you may ask happy customers to put pen to paper on your behalf as well.

If you want to gain a powerful testimonial letter from a satisfied customer, you may want to start by helping your customer to recall their satisfaction with your work. If someone has agreed to provide you with a testimonial, you may first want to consider engaging in the following conversation.

You may ask your customer, "What are the specific areas where my work with you (or the products you purchased from me) made a difference to you? How, specifically, did it make a difference?" Ask this for each area that comes up in the conversation.

If there are certain areas where the customer has expressed satisfaction or gratitude in the past, you may want to revisit these as well. For instance, "You mentioned in the past that the work we did together on your planning made a difference to your receivables. How specifically did this help you?"

For each area, after your customer finishes speaking to the difference that was made, ask this: "What was the impact of that on you (or on your business, or both)?" Another powerful question to ask is, "How does it make you feel when you see the impact that has been achieved?"

While your customer is speaking about these things, take point-form notes. List the various ways in which your products and/or services have made a difference to your customer. Then list the impact (and emotional consequences) left in each of those areas where differences were achieved.

When you are done with this, simply hand the sheet to your customer and ask for three things:

1. That the letter be addressed to you, and *not* "To Whom It May Concern,"
2. That the person identify the specifics of the difference that your products and/or services made,
3. The impact those differences made on the business, or on his/her life overall.

By providing that level of assistance to your happy customers, you will effectively avoid any possible requests for you to write something that you want that they sign and give it back to you (a definite no-no in testimonials!). Further, by assisting them in point form with some of the content for this letter, it is less likely to sit as a to-do on their desk, and more likely to gain the prompt treatment you hope for. You have made it easy for them to deal with this letter in a timely and complete fashion. Further, because your notes are in point form, your customer will write this letter in their own voice, which will have a stronger impact as a result.

5. Other Pertinent Materials

In addition to team credentials and customer testimonials, in some businesses the work may speak for itself. Advertising companies, cosmetic dentists, web design studios and construction/renovation companies all come to mind. These are businesses where you can visually measure the actual results of their work.

We had a kitchen cabinet designer as a client who always used before and after pictures to demonstrate the improvements to kitchens that their work achieved. This is routinely used by cosmetic surgeons, and weight-loss programs as well. When you show before and after pictures, you're visually defining the value of using your services.

To what extent do other pertinent materials apply to your business? These may well form a useful part of your marketing materials. I have found that for many service-based companies, case studies really draw out what can be achieved. Another kind of pertinent material is the "white paper". A white paper is an article indicating authority on a relevant subject.

Whether you use before and after pictures, case studies, white papers or some other pertinent material, these additions further strengthen your credibility with potential customers.

Summary

The five elements of marketing materials—your Credo, Process, Credentials, Testimonials and Other Pertinent Materials—can make a big difference in relationship development.

If you follow these guidelines, you will be on your way to building more effective marketing materials in support of the growth of your business, consistent with your goals and commitments in life.

CHAPTER 8

Organizational Structure

Organizational Structure

Thinking Through the Bigger Game

Most entrepreneurs don't realize that it is actually easier to double or triple in size than it is to have consistent and sustained 15% per year increases in sales. While this fact may surprise you, the reasoning will not.

As I mentioned earlier, productivity is a function of design and structure, not your good intent alone. Intent is necessary, but it is not enough to change the face of a business. To cause deep, lasting change, you need to develop a fundamentally different structure.

Well, that's all fine and good, but what's this about it being easier to double or triple than to go for more modest percentage increases in sales?

Normally, a business will gravitate to the level where it hits a natural limit in one or more areas. Sometimes it is in sales capacity. With one salesman, there are only so many orders that may be processed in a given period of time. Another area is delivery capacity. This is very common in an owner-operated professional service firm, whether it be a doctor's or dentist's office, a self-employed engineer, a small architecture firm, a massage therapist, a financial planner or some other professional practice. The owner's time is the issue, as he or she is part of the delivery mechanism. They are really good at what they do, and the customers want them personally, not some stand-in. So they have limits to their expansion possibilities, especially if they try to grow by only 15% per year.

Regardless of the type of business, if you try to pace your growth at about 15% per year, there are limits to what you can afford in infrastructure support. If I make $500,000 per year in a small, service-based business, then a 15% increase is $75,000 in gross sales. If I need labor support to deliver this, then it might well cost me an additional $40K to $50K to earn my $75K in sales. That only leaves me with $25K to $35K of additional gross profit. If I need new space to support the extra person, the costs start to add up to almost the same amount as the increase in revenues.

But what about my accounting system? How about the database? What about the additional marketing material that needs to be printed and the lead generation strategies that I need in order to attract the extra business? All of these factors spell additional costs. Instead, what you are likely to do is tighten the belt, work your existing people a little harder, and see how far you can stretch your existing resources.

And that is the problem with this type of growth. Your people get tired, mistakes start to occur, customer satisfaction declines, and you begin to wonder if it is worth it to try and grow at all. Still, you persevere, but with a little less energy than before, and though you muscle through, you don't get the satisfaction that you want to experience as a result of your growth.

If you knew you were going to double or triple—whether it took you one to two years or even three to four years—you probably wouldn't mind investing in the additional infrastructure, on a stepped or phased-in basis as needed, that would keep your people from becoming over-tired and you from risking burnout yourself. You wouldn't delude yourself into thinking the existing structures would continue to work, so your plans would include adding infrastructure for the higher levels of growth.

The Bigger Game

One of the critical elements of large-scale growth is to think through how the company will work at its larger size. In chapter 5, "Set Your Target", you set goals for the size of company you would like to build. This chapter asks you to plan your organizational structure for what it will need to look like when your company is growing to its target size.

Two areas where this will have obvious impacts will be your company's organization chart, and your company's financial statements. Let's start with the organization chart.

Your Organization Chart

As in most things regarding your organizational structure, you need to start with where you are currently. Your first task is to draw out your current organization chart. However, I would like you to do this in two ways:

1. Draw out your organization chart with all the names of your current employees and colleagues listed in the appropriate boxes.
2. Then, draw it out again, removing names and leaving only positions or titles in place in the squares.

Now set both these organization charts aside for the moment. We will return to them shortly.

Your next step is to draw out an organization chart, with titles or roles only, for the largest size of company you are contemplating. Let's say, for the purposes of this exercise, that you are currently at $1 million in sales, and your ultimate goal is to grow to $10 million in sales, with a targeted profit percentage. After drawing out two versions of your current organization chart (with and without the names), the next step is to draw out the chart at $10 million in sales.

Please see the example for a $10 million organization chart from an Architectural Technologist firm. It is critical that you think through your own $10 million chart before you scale back to smaller projections of your organization charts!

Example One: Organization Chart at $10 Million (120 People)

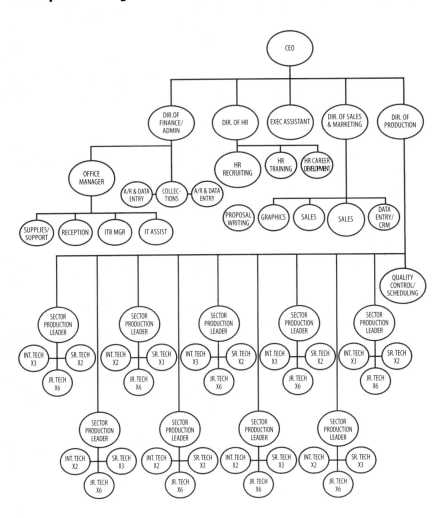

Looking at the $10 million organization chart raises a number of important questions: How will your company work at a size that is much larger than it is now? How will you deliver your goods and services to your customers at that size? What will be your geographic reach? Will you have more than one location? If so, where will your locations be? How will the logistics work? If you are dealing with hard goods, then how will they be transported? All these questions have an impact on your staffing levels, and on the costs involved in generating this level of sales.

Other questions to brainstorm include:

1. How will you be acquiring your sales? List this here.

_____
_____
_____
_____
_____
_____
_____
_____

2. Will you need a bigger sales force? How many new salespeople will you need? How will they be managed? Will you need sales supervisors, a sales manager, a series of regional managers, or some other structure of sales support?

_____
_____
_____
_____
_____
_____
_____
_____

3. Will you need customer service reps (or sales assistants) for each sales rep? How many will you need?

4. Will you need in-house marketing support? If so, what will the system look like? How will it work, and how many people will you need to make it work well at that level?

5. Speaking of people, what about your human resources department? At $1 million in sales you probably don't even have an HR department, but at $10 million, will you need one? If so, how many people will you need? What level of expertise will you need to hire? This will impact your costs, as well as the effectiveness of that department and how well staffed and profitable your other departments are.

6. How about your accounting and finance department? How many people will you have in this department? Will you be operating with a full CFO or will you be using a controller? How much strategy development will you be requiring from this person?

7. How deep will the accounting team be? Whether you are dealing mostly with larger dollar volume transactions or more with small ones will determine the number of invoices that go through your finance department, and may have a significant impact on your staffing needs. Will you need a separate purchaser, or will that be part of someone's role?

8. What about administrative support? Who will need it, and at what levels? Will you have shared admin support, or dedicated? Who gets dedicated support, and for what activities?

9. How will your production services work? What levels of supervision will be needed to make them work, but also still keep them profitable?

10. What about training? How much training will the people in each of the departments need? Who will be providing the training support? How much of that will be in-house training, and how much will be outsourced? Who will actually do the training? How does this impact your numbers of staff?

11. What about personal and professional career development for your staff? Will that be part of what you will be offering to attract and retain top employees? How will it work? What level of staff support will be needed?

12. What I.T. support will be needed? Will it be in-house or outsourced? How many computers will you have at $10 million? How often will they need to be updated or replaced?

13. In addition to your salespeople, will you need an internal estimating or proposal development department? If so, how will it be staffed? If not, how will you manage proposals and quotes?

_____
_____
_____
_____
_____
_____

Needless to say, there are a great many variables involved in thinking through the bigger game. All these questions will impact your organization chart at $10 million in revenues. However, the good news is that this is the bulk of the work you will need to do. After you have answered these questions, you will be armed with what you need to draw out the organization chart at $10 million in revenues. I offer these questions for you in a format that will allow you to just write out the answers, so that you may then proceed to drawing your organization chart.

In addition to these questions, I have included an outline for developing a business plan report (see below). This outline, adapted from one I received from one of my professors during my MBA studies, is the most thorough yet effective summary that I have come across in my professional career. By thinking each component through, even at a cursory level, you will gain further insight into how to build out an organization chart, as well as other valuable aspects of your company, which will guide you on what you might expect at $10 million in sales.

Outline for a Complete Business Plan Report

1. Executive summary
2. Identification of the product(s) and/or service(s) to be offered by the company, including the essential specifications and rationale, and the country or countries with which the company will trade (3–5 pages)
3. Policies guiding selection of products and/or services (a summary of the policies used in guiding the selection of products and/or services and the countries with which the company will trade) (2–4 pages)
4. Vision statement (a summary of the strategic vision of the company, e.g. uniqueness, long-term ambition, competitive advantage, strategic concept, etc.) (2–4 pages)
5. Mission, objectives and policies of the company (3–5 pages)
6. Organization and management of the company (type of company, legal basis, ownership, organization chart, etc.) (4–6 pages)
7. Main assumptions of company operations for the next five years (economic, legal, political, resources, technological, competitive, etc.) (3–5 pages)
8. Physical requirements for the next five years (location(s), plant and equipment, offices, furnishing, plant and/or office layout, etc.) (4–6 pages)
9. Plan to establish company's next specific level of growth (flowchart of steps required, timetable, etc.) (3–4 pages)
10. Production plan for the next five years (all aspects of manufacturing or processing relevant to the products to be offered, to the extent this is applicable) (5–7 pages)
11. Marketing plan for the next five years (marketing plan for the company, including target markets, research and analysis, advertising, promotion, pricing, etc.) (4–5 pages)
12. Information plan for the next five years (decision support systems, internal and external communication, etc.) (4–5 pages)
13. Human resources plan for the next five years (numbers and types of staff members, job outlines for all technical, management and

professional staff, full staffing plan, remuneration plan, etc.) (4–6 pages)
14. Financial plan for the next five years (sources and costs of capital, funding mechanism requested (if any), cash flow projection, pro forma profit and loss statement, etc.) (4–6 pages)

The Financial Statements

After completing a first draft of an organization chart, you will next need to work through and do some math to figure out if you can afford all the people you are planning for. In order to do that, you will need to build an Income Statement for your projected growth(our example, for the purposes of this exercise, involves $10 million in gross sales).

The Income Statement: Elements to Consider

There are a number of elements to include in this Income Statement. Start with your current Income Statement and use the categories that you now have, updating the numbers for your projected increase in sales (a ten-fold increase, for the purposes of our example). In particular, you will want to calculate the following:

- The breakdown of where (from what products, services and/or geographic locations) your sales come from—what will your new, bigger company's sales comprise?
- The cost of sales in each product or service category
- Your gross profit levels, overall and by department/product/service

- Your fixed expenses, namely:
  - Facilities
  - Equipment leases
  - Staff wages, employee benefits, payroll taxes, worker's compensation, etc.
  - Vehicle expenses
  - Transport costs
  - Costs of any lines of credit you need to carry accounts receivable
  - Credit card merchant costs
  - Hiring costs, training costs
  - Management bonuses, staff bonuses
  - All your other fixed expenses
- Desired Net Income levels

From all this, you will be able to do a reality check to see if you caught all the main items that you will likely face. Then, when you have completed this step, bring your numbers to your accountant or your business advisor. Get their take on things. We not only help people to review this type of planning, we actually get involved in helping to build out the models. It is quite a lot of work, so it never hurts to get an outside set of eyes on your plans.

After completing the Income Statement, either by yourself or with the help of your accountant or business advisor, figure out what your Balance Sheet will need to look like at that level.

The Balance Sheet: Elements to Consider

The purpose in completing a Balance Sheet at $10 million is to think through your capital needs at that level. What are the capital assets you will need in order to operate at that size? For example, two partners who are clients of ours are in the commercial air conditioning business. Two aspects of their business that affect their

Balance Sheet are their parts inventory and their fleet of service vehicles.

How much inventory does each service technician need onboard their truck? How many trucks will be in the fleet? How long will each vehicle be in the fleet before it is replaced? Will the vehicles be leased or purchased? If purchased, how will the company pay for them? From profits? By borrowing? A combination? If a combination, what will be the breakdown between cash and borrowing? How will this be funded?

Another area to consider is how you will be funding any accounts receivable you may have at $10 million in sales. What are your current terms with customers? Will that change as you grow? How much short-term access to cash (either through financial reserves or a line of credit) will you need?

All these questions support you in gaining the clarity you will need to grow. If you need help with this, ask your accountant or your business advisor. He/she will be happy to assist you with this step.

Scaling Down the Model

Once you are happy with the preliminary model you have developed (the organization chart, the Income Statement and the Balance Sheet), then it is time to take the next step. That is, to scale down the model—to develop interim goals to achieve. In our example, a $1 million company seeking to go to $10 million, the first scaled-down version I would recommend would be $5 million. Build out the organization chart (again, with positions, but not names) for $5 million. After that, you will want to build out the Income Statement and Balance Sheet for $5 million as well.

After completing these steps for $5 million, the next step is to do the same thing for $2 million in sales. Build out the organization chart for $2 million, and then the Income Statement and Balance Sheet for $2 million as well. By building out first the $10 million organization chart and financial statements, and then going to the $5 million, followed by the $2 million, you will make sure that the smaller company structures are going to dovetail into what you will ultimately need for the $10 million company.

One of the biggest mistakes people make when taking on large-scale growth is to start at the present ($1 million) and then go to $2 million, followed by $5 million and then on to $10 million. This means the limitations that you see at $2 million will impact your $5 million and $10 million plans. Better to start by thinking through the $10 million picture, and then stepping it back to $5 million, and only after you have both, draw out the $2 million chart and numbers. This vastly increases your chances of generating a truly integrated plan that will be much easier to achieve.

You'll next find an example of a scaled-down $5 million version of the $10 million dollar organization chart.

Example Two: Organization Chart for $5Million (66 people)

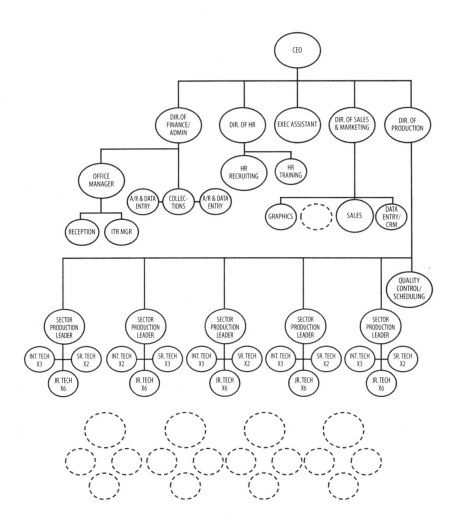

Building the Transition Plan

The transitional organization chart (in this case, for $2 million) is the one that you will work with to develop your transitional strategy from where you are now to where you want to go (see Example Three).

With both the current organization chart (with names) and the one for $2 million in front of you, start to evaluate the people you currently have on your team. For each person, ask yourself the following:

- What is the growth potential of this person?
- Where is he/she likely to grow to on this org. chart?
- Are there any limitations this person has that might limit future growth?
- How well does this person fit into my current org. chart?
- How likely will it be that this person will fit into the company as it grows? In what position?

At this point you really need to tell the truth about your people. By identifying possible limitations, or possible opportunities for growth, you can now test people as you go, to see where in fact they will fit into the company as it expands.

This step is critical for your lasting success. If you check in now, as you are looking to grow, you can watch your people, encourage their development, and see where they bring themselves within your company. Don't be surprised if you find that one or more don't quite fit, and either quit or you need to let them go. This is the worst part of having a business, but it is part of having a business, and it must be addressed. There is very little in life more expensive than having the wrong people in the wrong roles within your company.

Of course, before letting someone go, you may want to check to see if there is another role, as you grow, where this person may be a good fit.

Once you are clear on what roles people might fit into as you evolve from your $1 million company into a $2 million firm, you will have also identified the roles that will need to be filled as you grow into these numbers. Set your priorities for the order of hiring new people, and start.

One key here is to tie the hiring events with other events within the company. For example, you may decide to go find a new salesperson immediately. However, you may wait until that person is with you and producing before adding an additional customer service representative (or inside sales support person). By staging your hiring to coincide with events in your business, rather than tying them to preset timelines, you will have the flexibility to allow your business to evolve at an appropriate rate, rather than force a level of growth when you are not ready. From there, take things one step at a time, and adjust (constantly) along the way.

If you take the time to work through the planning in this section, you will find that you will be rewarded dramatically for your efforts. By breaking things down into these components, the apparently insurmountable task of large-scale growth becomes manageable. Instead of fearing it, you will grow to enjoy the process as well as the challenges that it brings.

Example Three: Organization Chart for $2Million (26 people)

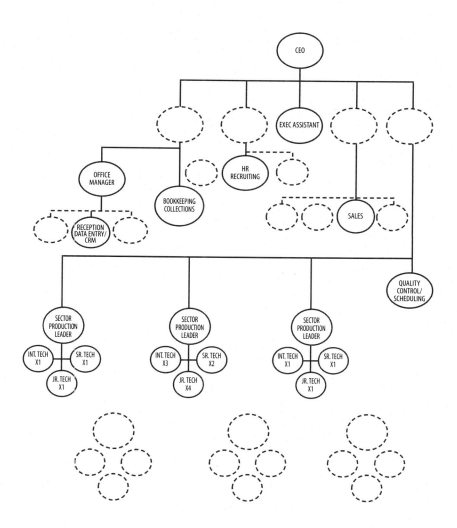

CHAPTER 9

Cash Flow

Cash Flow

A discussion of structures for the growth of your company would not be complete without including a plan for your cash flow. Profit is important, but in a growing business, cash is king. Growing costs money and it will eat up your cash if you are not careful. There are many issues to address, and many strategies to address them.

The core tool to be developed and utilized is the cash flow forecast. This is a very powerful measuring tool that looks forward into the near future of your business, rather than merely looking back at the past. Before we get to a cash flow forecast, we need to take a step back and review how the Income Statement works to give you the information you will need in order to develop a useful forecast that will support you in moving forward. To do this, let's review the concept of backward pricing.

How do you generate the results that you want in your business? The first key to success is to develop a set of measures. What are the areas of importance within your organization? It has been said that if you cannot measure it, you cannot manage it. If you cannot manage it, you don't control it. If you don't control it, how much do you want to invest in it? Yet, in business we see well-intended efforts that don't yield results so frequently that you would think that this is the way business is supposed to be.

Measuring: The Income Statement

What do you measure? Let's start with some basics. The income statement of a business generally starts by showing how much you generate in overall revenues. This we will refer to as Gross Sales.

You then deduct the direct costs associated with your product/service that have only been incurred directly as a result of the sales you generated. These are called Cost of Goods Sold (or COGS for short). Examples of COGS include materials costs, direct labor incurred and any special outsourced costs you spend, such as shipping. By deducting COGS from Gross Sales, you identify the Gross Profit.

Meet Joe. He owns a small manufacturing facility in Small Town, USA. He has been operating there for years, and here are brief summaries of some of the numbers from his most recent monthly Income Statement.

Gross Sales	$120,000	100%
Less: COGS	$80,000	67%
Gross Profit	$40,000	33%

In Joe's example, 67% of the Gross Sales are needed to cover direct costs (or COGS), leaving 33%, or $40,000, available to Joe to pay the rest of his bills.

Next, Joe has to pay his fixed expenses. These are the other expenses of the company, which generally do not change substantially with increases and decreases in sales. These include rent, administrative wages, utilities, leases, etc. If you need to pay it each month, whether your sales volume is high or low, chances are it falls into this category.

What are your fixed expenses? How much Gross Profit do you need to generate to pay all your bills each month? This is another critical piece of the puzzle. Once clarified, you may then calculate how much money you are making for You. In Joe's case, the numbers continue as follows:

Gross Profit	$40,000
Fixed Expenses	-$38,000
Net Income (before taxes)	$ 2,000

In this case, any Gross Profit in excess of $38,000 generates positive net income for Joe's company. Note: the $38,000 income number includes Joe's pay and all other expenses that the company incurs each month.

Backward Pricing

Backward pricing is a method of clarifying what you want from your business, and what it will take to get it. The notion is to start with your intended results and work backwards to calculate what it would take to get what you want. Using the scenario above, let's walk through the concept of backward pricing.

Steps

1. CLARIFY YOUR FINANCIAL GOALS

What are your financial goals for the company? Do you want to make $50,000 this year (after expenses)? $100,000? $1 million? You are the one who gets to say what you want. After you figure out what it might take to accomplish your goal, you may go back and adjust it later. For the purposes of our exercise, let's say that Joe wants to generate a Net Income (before taxes) of $180,000 over the course of the year. This translates into an average monthly profit of $15,000 per month.

2. DETERMINE GROSS PROFIT NEEDED

Once you have set your goal, then work backwards (hence the term "Backward Pricing"). In order to achieve $15,000 in profits, Joe will need to generate $53,000 in Gross Profit each month.

Gross Profit	$53,000
Less: Fixed Expenses	-$38,000
Net Income (before tax)	$15,000

3. DETERMINE GROSS SALES NEEDED

To generate $53,000 in Gross Profit, Joe will need a total of $159,000 each month in Gross Sales.

Gross Sales	$159,000	100%
Less: COGS	-$106,000	67%
Gross Profit	$53,000	33%

If Joe generates Gross Sales of $159,000 per month, then this will be a total of $1,908,000 per year.

To summarize, Joe needs to build his company sales levels to just over $1.9 million to achieve his financial goal of $180,000 net income before tax.

Purpose of the Cash Flow Forecast

There are a number of purposes for the cash flow forecast. The primary two purposes are:

1. To anticipate what to expect in the coming year, so that you can plan accordingly
2. To measure the consequences of change

One thing we know is that life will unfold differently from the predictions on your cash flow forecast. We just don't know how, specifically, they will be different. By measuring your actual performance against the forecast, you will be able to make informed decisions on adjustments needed as you go through the year.

The first step to building a cash flow forecast is to refer to the monthly Income Statement that you assembled in the section entitled "Your Profit". This will be the basis of your forecast. Like your monthly Income Statements, the cash flow forecast may be developed in Excel.

Microsoft Office Excel

Warning: We are about to enter the world of Excel and numbers again. Even though this is a critical and necessary step, not everyone is good at Excel, and many entrepreneurs claim to be no good at their own numbers.

If you don't know how to use Excel, do not fret. You may want to find someone who is conversant with Excel to help you. This is not necessarily the time to learn a new program. There are many people who are very good with Excel (it is a very popular program within the Microsoft Office suite of software products). As a result, you should not find it difficult to gain access to this level of help.

If you don't have any friends or colleagues to help, or if you feel uncomfortable showing others in your company your numbers, you may always call one of the local temp services and ask them to send you a temp who knows Excel. This way, you can keep your confidentiality and get the job done as well. If you watch the person inputting, and get them to show you how basic formulas work (copy, paste and auto-sum are the features you will use the most with this forecast), then you will probably be able to update this on your own, or through your own bookkeeper, moving forward, once the basic spreadsheet is set up.

Important Note

Regarding your numbers, it is critical that you understand your money to be successful in business. Financial profit to a business is like eating is to life. There is much more to life than eating—unless you are starving! No matter how well you have managed the eating thing, notice that you still need to address it every single day. Skip a week and you may not be around to see what happens next. The problem with financial profit in a business is that people think that it is a good thing to go after, rather than a critical element that must be addressed every single day and week, just like eating, for your business to survive!

A business is about much more than financial profit, just like life is about much more than eating. Yet, without financial profit, there is no business. Let's get really clear about this. This is not some money-hungry pitch to change your values. This is a reality check: No financial profit = No business. It is as plain as that.

As a result, you need to become familiar with your numbers in order to grow effectively. Hence the need to work through the financial forecast yourself, rather than merely delegating this particular task. Now, on to the task of setting up Excel to work through this exercise.

Setting Up Excel

Within a new Excel worksheet, line up your columns so that column A is thirty units wide and B through N are each fourteen units wide. You can always adjust the column widths later if you need to, but I find that these are good widths to start. Beginning in cell B1, enter the first month of your spreadsheet (for example, if you are in February, then you may set your first month as March and do your forecast for March through to the following February). You want to set this up so that your first month is next month, and then go for twelve consecutive months. For our purposes, I will assume we are doing this in November, and so we will run the cash flow forecast from December through to the following November.

This is consistent with the example that comes later in this segment. It is not important that you start with January, unless you are building this in December. The key is to address the next twelve months, whatever they are.

Then, down column A, list all the categories that are currently in your Income Statement (starting at cell A2. By the time you are finished, your cash flow forecast will look similar to your monthly income statement, with no numbers filled in yet.

Populating the Numbers

The first area to address is your regular monthly expenses (similar to the fixed expenses we referred to in the "Backward Pricing" segment). Go through and list the expenses that you know you will be incurring, and which don't change much on a monthly basis. Things like rent, telephone, other utilities, Internet service, supplies, equipment leases; basically, all the things that are regular and predictable.

Special Note

Some places charge for service every two months rather than monthly—for example, some utilities in a home-based business. If that is the case, then list those expenses every other month, in the month where you expect to pay them, rather than averaging the numbers out to a monthly equivalent. The closer we set this to real life, the more useful it will be.

Within the expenses there will be categories that need to be broken down into more detail than your Income Statement may show. For example, vehicle expenses may be shown as one number on your Income Statement, when that number is the composite of a whole bunch of numbers.

In our example at the end of this section, the company is paying for five different vehicles. There is a one-ton truck, a van, a Sundance, a Ford Escape (vehicles of the husband and wife, who are the owners) and a forklift. For each vehicle, the expenses are broken down in detail as applicable, listing the anticipated costs for the lease payment (or interest on car payment, as applicable), insurance, gas and oil, parking, licence and permits, and repairs and maintenance. What is the purpose of this? If these people sold one vehicle, or replaced it with a newer one, they could very quickly see the specific financial consequences.

The utility of this forecast is contingent on how detailed you make it as you fill it out. Please make it as detailed as possible, as it will make a big difference to you throughout the year.

Staff Wages

One of the beautiful things about Excel is that you can hide and unhide rows (and columns, too). This comes in handy when we are looking at staff costs. I recommend that you break down your staff costs by person, listing each person in your company separately, each person in their own separate row, putting in their monthly wages as applicable. Then you can put in a summary for payroll taxes (in the USA) or EI and CPP (in Canada). Employee benefits I usually put in as a summarized number in its own row, unless I am dealing with a very small company with fewer than ten or twelve people in the USA, where health insurance is very expensive and varies widely between and among respective employees of differing ages. Then I track it separately—one row per employee. You can decide what is useful to you. Remember, the important thing is: Are the numbers you are entering an accurate estimate of what is to come? If so, you are in good shape.

Another advantage to breaking out the staff wages is that you can add a separate row for each of the new staff you anticipate hiring in the coming year, as established when you worked through the exercises in the organizational structure part of this system. If you know you will be adding one new production person every three months, then you can actually put this person's income into your forecast and see the consequences of this new additional expense on your monthly cash flow. You may then adjust things if events dictate that you hire more quickly, more slowly, or if you have to replace someone.

After you have completed the expenses in the first month, copy and paste the appropriate cells into the subsequent months for each row, as applicable.

Totaling the Expenses

Once you have all the monthly expense numbers inputted, add the totals at the bottom to see what your basic monthly financial expenses will be for each month of the coming year. Add to this number the amount you wish to earn each month over the course of the year (separate row—often referred to as the Target Net Income). The two combined form the Gross Profit that you will need to achieve to reach your goals (consistent with our previously mentioned "backward pricing" example for Joe's business).

Gross Sales, Cost of Sales and Gross Profit

Once you have calculated the Gross Profit (GP) you need to generate to pay your monthly bills and meet your personal income goals, you will need to calculate the Gross Sales you need to generate in order to pay your direct costs and meet your targets for GP. Calculate what percentage of your sales (from your past Income Statements) form your direct costs, so that you will have a formula similar to the one used in Joe's example. In Joe's case, his direct costs were 67% of Gross Sales. So, for every dollar in Gross Profit, Joe needs $3 in Gross Sales. What is your ratio? What has it been over the last year? Is it likely to change? Calculate this for yourself and then you can set your sales targets accordingly. Once you have those numbers, populate the top portion of your cash flow forecast for the year.

What if the numbers are unrealistically high (or low)? Then now is the time to adjust them. While you may want a certain net income from your business, it may take you a while to develop your sales to achieve these goals. Give yourself the time to work into the strategies you will need to achieve your sales objectives. Even if it takes three to six months, it is worth setting goals you can believe, and you can deliver.

Capital Expenditures

There are a couple of other elements to a cash flow forecast that make it different from an Income Statement. Below the Net Income line in our example at the end of this section, you will notice a series of rows for other capital expenditures. This includes payments you make to pay down principal on loans, any capital expenses you incur to buy things for the business, and other such items that impact your cash flow, but not your Income Statement.

Below the Net Income per month line, you will notice in the example a Cumulative Net Income line. By tracking this, you will be able to see whether you will need financing to support your cash flow during any periods of the year. Then, after the principal pay-down section, there is a net cash flow surplus/deficit followed by a cumulative cash flow surplus/deficit row. With the additional information you gain from these extra rows, you can address your banking and borrowing needs well in advance of actually needing the funds. A loan or increase on a line of credit is generally far easier to obtain in advance rather than when you actually need the money.

Uses for the Cash Flow Forecast

Once you have set up your numbers, and you feel they are realistic, you will have the information on what targets you need to reach in order to achieve your goals. From there you will be setting your sales and production strategies, and getting into action.

The cash flow forecast is a very effective tool to support you in doing that initial reality check. However, its utility does not stop there. As you unfold your strategies, you will be able to measure your effectiveness on your financial situation simply by inputting the actual results into your forecast on a month-by-month basis.

In the case of the company in the example, they had gotten themselves into a bit of a financial squeeze, and the cash flow forecast allowed them to watch and see if any surpluses were coming in each month so that they could get a handle on their debt and pay it down in an orderly fashion. This turned out to be a very effective strategy, and though it took some time to accomplish, the owners started to sleep better at night, rather than feel the burdens of their financial difficulties.

By building and using the cash flow forecast, you will be better positioned to clarify, develop and roll out your growth strategies, armed with a measurement tool that will support you in conducting the ongoing reality check that you will need in order to accomplish your business goals.

Example: Cash Flow Forecast

	December	January	February	March	April	May	June	July	August	September	October	November	Total	Average
Anticipated Revenues (after discounts)	85,000	121,000	107,000	104,000	100,000	102,000	99,000	101,000	107,000	101,000	100,000	100,000	1,227,000	102,250
Warehouse Revenues	10,000	10,000	10,000	10,000	10,000	10,000	10,000	10,000	10,000	10,000	10,000	10,000	120,000	10,000
Merchandise Sales-Steelcase	34,650												34,650	2,887
Total Revenues	129,650	131,000	117,000	114,000	110,000	112,000	109,000	111,000	117,000	111,000	110,000	110,000	1,381,650	115,137
Cost of Goods Sold														
Direct Labour	55,250	78,650	69,550	67,600	65,000	66,300	64,350	65,650	69,550	65,650	65,000	65,000	797,550	66,462
WCB (direct)	3,867	5,505	4,868	4,732	4,550	4,641	4,504	4,595	4,868	4,595	4,550	4,550	55,828	4,652
Supplier Pay Down - 2nd Bridge Loan	17,000												17,000	1,416
Total Cost of Goods Sold	76,117	84,155	74,418	72,332	69,550	70,941	68,854	70,245	74,418	70,245	69,550	69,550	870,378	72,531
Gross Margin	53,532	46,844	42,581	41,668	40,450	41,059	40,145	40,754	42,581	40,754	40,450	40,450	511,271	42,605
EXPENSES														
Rent	8,975	8,975	8,975	8,975	8,975	8,975	8,975	8,975	8,975	8,975	8,975	8,975	107,700	8,975
Payroll														
The Two Owners	5,590	5,590	5,590	5,590	5,590	5,590	5,590	5,590	5,590	5,590	5,590	5,590	67,080	5,590
Dispatcher (salary-9 hr days)	1,500	3,000	3,000	3,000	3,000	3,000	3,000	3,000	3,000	3,000	3,000	3,000	34,500	2,875
Admin Clerk (12.50)	1,950	1,950	1,950	1,950	1,950	1,950	1,950	1,950	1,950	1,950	1,950	1,950	23,400	1,950
Book keeper (2 d/w @ 15)		1,200	1,200	800	800	800	800	800	800	800	800	800	9,600	800
Warehouseman (12)	2,100	2,100	2,100	2,100	2,100	2,100	2,100	2,100	2,100	2,100	2,100	2,100	25,200	2,100
Payroll Expenses (WCB in)	1,349	1,517	1,517	1,461	1,461	1,461	1,461	1,461	1,461	1,461	1,461	1,461	17,539	1,461
RRSP	100	100	100	100	100	100	100	100	100	100	100	100	1,200	100
Subcontractors [whse,etc] (WCB in)	1,000	1,000	1,000	1,000	1,000	1,000	1,000	1,000	1,000	1,000	1,000	1,000	12,000	1,000

Example: Cash Flow Forecast (continued)

	December	January	February	March	April	May	June	July	August	September	October	November	Total	Average
Vehicle Costs														
1 Ton														
Lease (ends Mar/02)	665	665	665	665									2,660	221
Insurance	130	130	130	130	130	130	130	130	130	130	130	130	1,564	130
Gas (card 4) [average-all vehicles]	1,500	1,500	1,500	1,500	1,500	1,500	1,500	1,500	1,500	1,500	1,500	1,500	18,000	1,500
Repair & Maintenance (500/yr)			500										500	41
Parking	30	30	30	30	30	30	30	30	30	30	30	30	360	30
Licensing & Permits (60/yr)				60									60	5
Van														
Insurance	99	99	99	99	99	99	99	99	99	99	99	99	1,196	99
Gas (card various)													.	
Repair & Maintenance				300									300	25
Parking	30	30	30	30	30	30	30	30	30	30	30	30	360	30
Licensing & Permits				60									60	5
Sundance														
Insurance	100	100	100	100	100	100	100	100	100	100	100	100	1,200	100
Gas (card 1)													.	
Repair & Maintenance		300											300	25
Parking	50	50	50	50	50	50	50	50	50	50	50	50	600	50
Licensing & Permits				60									60	5
Ford Escape														
Payment	760	760	760	760	760	760	760	760	760	760	760	760	9,131	760
Insurance							130	130	130	130	130		650	54
Repair & Maintenance						500							500	41
Parking													.	.
Licensing & Permits							50						50	4
Forklift														
Lease (ends june/03)	257	257	257	257	257	257	257	257	257	257	257	257	3,087	257
Repair & Maintenance				150						150			300	25
Gas	15	15	15	15	15	15	15	15	15	15	15	15	180	15

Example: Cash Flow Forecast (continued)

	December	January	February	March	April	May	June	July	August	September	October	November	Total	Average
Loan Financing - Interest														
Line of Credit	300	300	300	300	300	300	300	300	300	300	300	300	3,600	300
Mastercard	88	79	68	58	48	37	27	16	5	-	-	-	430	35
Supplier 1 Bridge Loan	200	200	200	200	200	200	200	200	200	200	200	200	2,400	200
Supplier 1 Discount Loan													-	-
Second Bridge Loan	310	168	168	168	168	168	168	168	168	168	168	168	2,158	179
Other														
Office Supplies	100	100	400	400	400	400	400	400	400	400	400	400	4,200	350
Warehouse Supplies	40	40	40	40	40	40	40	40	40	40	40	40	480	40
Accounting	3,000	3,000	500	500	500	500	500	500	500	500	500	500	11,000	916
Automated Invoice/Dispatch System (12k)	500	500	500	500	500	500	500	500	500	500	500	500	6,000	500
Legal													-	-
Advertising & Promotion														
Dominion Directories	32	32	32	32	32	32	32	32	32	32	32	32	384	32
CW													-	-
General Insurance		2,000											2,000	166
Business Coaching	1,800	1,800	1,800	1,800	1,800	1,800	1,800	1,800	1,800	1,800	1,800	1,800	21,600	1,800
Waste Disposal	50	300	50	300	50	300	50	300	50	300	50	300	2,100	175
Office Water	50	50	50	50	50	50	50	50	50	50	50	50	600	50
Company functions	2,500							2,500					5,000	416
Meals & Entertainment	200	200	200	200	200	200	200	200	200	200	200	200	2,400	200
Utilities	800	800	800	400	400	400	250	250	250	250	400	400	5,400	450
Telephone	300	300	300	300	300	300	300	300	300	300	300	300	3,600	300
Cell phones	1,000	1,000	1,000	1,000	1,000	1,000	1,000	1,000	1,000	1,000	1,000	1,000	12,000	1,000
Licenses & Permits		100											100	8
Computer Technician	200	200	200										600	50
Miscellaneous	100	100	100	100	100	100	100	100	100	100	100	100	1,200	100
Tickets & Fines		100		100		100		100					500	41
Total Expenses	38,154	40,820	36,359	35,473	34,418	34,957	33,947	34,466	36,555	34,549	34,199	34,449	428,352	35,696
Net Monthly Income/ (Loss)	15,377	6,024	6,221	6,194	6,031	6,101	6,198	6,288	6,026	6,204	6,250	6,000	82,918	6,909
Cumulative Net Profit/ (Loss)	15,377	21,402	27,623	33,818	39,849	45,951	52,149	58,437	64,463	70,668	76,918	82,918		

Example: Cash Flow Forecast (continued)

	December	January	February	March	April	May	June	July	August	September	October	November	Total	Average
Loan Financing - Payments														
Line of Credit														
MasterCard	661	670	681	691	701	712	722	733	744	355				
Supplier 1 Bridge Loan														
Supplier 1 Discount Loan														
Second Bridge Loan														
Total Debt Payments	661	670	681	691	701	712	722	733	744	355	-	-		
Net Cash Flow Surplus/ Deficit	14,716	5,353	5,540	5,503	5,330	5,389	5,475	5,554	5,281	5,849	6,250	6,000	76,243	
Cumulative Cash Flow/ Deficit	14,716	20,070	25,610	31,113	36,443	41,832	47,308	52,863	58,144	63,993	70,243	76,243		
Loan Financing - Balances														
Line of Credit	25,000	25,000	25,000	25,000	25,000	25,000	25,000	25,000	25,000	25,000	25,000	25,000		
Mastercard	5,930	5,268	4,597	3,916	3,225	2,524	1,811	1,089	355	-	-	-		
Supplier 1 Bridge Loan	20,000	20,000	20,000	20,000	20,000	20,000	20,000	20,000	20,000	20,000	20,000	20,000		
Supplier 1 Discount Loan	30,000	30,000	30,000	30,000	30,000	30,000	30,000	30,000	30,000	30,000	30,000	30,000		
Second Bridge Loan	37,000	20,000	20,000	20,000	20,000	20,000	20,000	20,000	20,000	20,000	20,000	20,000		
Total Financing Balances	117,930	100,268	99,597	98,916	98,225	97,524	96,811	96,089	95,355	95,000	95,000	95,000		

CHAPTER 10

Pulling It All Together

Pulling It All Together

Intended Outcomes Revisited

We have gone over a great number of elements that are critical to achieving large-scale growth in your business. The purpose of this summary is to pull together the various pieces of the puzzle, so that we may meet the intended outcomes that were stated in the Introduction.

In the Introduction to this book, I stated three specific intended outcomes. They were:

1. to give you clear, practical advice to access your own personal power and creative energy to achieve large-scale growth in your business;
2. to help you to clarify how much growth to aspire to; and
3. to guide you in building a game plan for large-scale growth in your business.

Outcome 1

To give you clear, practical access to tap your own personal power and creative energy to achieve large-scale growth in your business.

The first step to gaining functional access to tap your own personal power and creative energy is to take time off. By treating self-care as a priority, you will be more refreshed and have all of your energy available to you as you work through the process of growing your business. Remember to take time off before getting into the Problem Zone, so that you may consistently tap increased clarity and creativity and attend to the tasks associated with growth.

Related to the first step is to actively risk manage your capacity levels. By handling and monitoring your foundation items, by making sure you have adequate personal space and by setting up your personal money to avoid worry, you will be protecting your confidence levels, which will be vital to your growth.

Adopt the philosophy of kaizen, which means incremental growth or continual improvement. By taking things one step at a time, you will find yourself moving through the steps to grow your business faster than you had imagined.

By clarifying for yourself where you spend your time, and by identifying which activities you can delegate to others, you will be freed up to take on the strategies and tasks that will catapult your business forward in service of your goals.

These steps will provide you with increased access to your own personal power, a vital element of achieving large-scale growth in your business.

Outcome 2

To clarify how much growth to aspire to and how to line it up so that it gives you what you want.

In the chapter of this guide on setting your target, we first reviewed the anatomy of effective goals. Then, we discussed questions relating to:

- What you want personally
- What level of professional growth and development you seek
- How your business might provide personal and professional growth
- What level of business you really want

HOW MUCH GROWTH IS APPROPRIATE FOR YOU?

Only you can say for sure. It really is up to you to answer these questions. I can help you clarify what you want, but at the end of the day, you want to set up your business to serve your goals. Having said that, the series of questions provided in the "Set Your Target" section of this book will assist you to think through what's important to you, and how big to grow your business in service of your goals and commitments.

If you haven't yet worked through these questions, take the time to do so, and really think them through. Even if you are clear on what you want, these questions will help you to gain further clarity on a number of dimensions, both what you want personally, and what needs to be present in your business to achieve your corporate goals.

Outcome 3

To guide you in building a game plan to structure your business for large-scale growth.

To this end, I have provided a number of steps, which are summarized as follows:

Review the "Criteria for Large-Scale Growth" in chapter 2. If you are unsure of whether any of these are missing, or are inadequate, please use the valuable tools that were provided to help you shore up those areas, so that you are ready to grow.

Clarify your current and recent profitability. You do this by attending to the following:

YOUR PROFIT

1. Collect your financial information.
2. Organize your financial statements in Excel so they are easier to analyze.

3. Work with your accountant for the following steps if you need to. If you don't have a good accountant, get one.
4. Analyze your Income Statements and Balance Sheets, past and present, using the questions I have provided as a guideline.
5. Analyze your customer list, breaking it down into quintiles. Identify the relevant trends.
6. From these analyses, determine who you will be targeting as customers as you grow, and what products/services you will be focusing upon to achieve your goals for growth.

CUSTOMER VALUE

1. Clarify and deepen your value proposition, your clarity of the value you provide for customers, and how you communicate that to them.
2. Build your Credo.
3. Clarify your processes for generating customer results and label them.
4. Crystallize for yourself the customer experience of value that you desire that people receive from your business.
5. Confirm the actual level of customer satisfaction, and just what the current level of value is, by conducting customer satisfaction surveys.
6. Pull together or update your marketing materials, including your Credo, Process, Credentials, Testimonials and other pertinent material for use with new potential customers.

ORGANIZATIONAL STRUCTURE

1. Think through the bigger game of your future larger company.
2. Draw two different organization charts for your current company – one with employee names and one with roles only.
3. Address all the questions posed within the guide and in the business plan outline in order to clarify the various dimensions of your future, bigger company.
4. Draw the organization chart for the largest size of company you can see yourself owning.

5. Next, build out the Income Statement and the Balance Sheet for the company at that size, taking into account all the variables that you considered.
6. After you are satisfied with the results of #4 and #5 above, draw out the organization chart and develop the Income Statements and Balance Sheets for two interim target sales levels for the company.
7. Using the current organization chart and the one for the next level, develop the transition plan for staff.
8. Evaluate your current staff to determine their potential ability to grow into the future roles you will need in the organization.
9. Build a plan to hire people to fill the new roles on a staged basis as the company grows.

CASH FLOW

1. Develop and use a cash flow forecast as a measuring tool.
2. Review the information and example on backward pricing.
3. Following the steps provided, develop your cash flow forecast for the next twelve months.
4. Include in the forecast any anticipated changes that you will be implementing (including hiring, etc.).
5. As you unfold your strategies, update your cash flow forecast with actual numbers on a monthly basis and make adjustments for any changes that come along as your company evolves.

These steps, if followed, will provide you with the foundational structures you need to achieve large-scale growth. However, an important point to remember is that life rewards action. What you know is nice, but it is what you DO that counts. By following these steps, you will have a firm structural foundation on which to grow your business—one that is consistent with your goals and commitments in life.

This may sound like a lot to accomplish, and it is. Let's not kid ourselves. If it were easy, everyone would be doing it. Give yourself time. You don't have to do it all at once (even though many entrepreneurs want to do just that!). If you take things one step at a time, consistent with the notion of kaizen, you will build the business of your dreams in service of your goals and commitments in life.

45-Point Checklist: Strategies for Large-Scale Growth

This book is a strategic guide that has taken you through a great number of elements that are critical to achieving large-scale growth in your business. The purpose of this checklist is to pull together the various pieces of the puzzle, so that you may more easily accomplish the "Intended Outcomes" that were stated in the Introduction. The following steps, if followed, will provide you with the foundational structures you need to achieve large-scale growth. Remember, you don't have to do them all at once. Just start with three to five of these, and then come back and choose three to five more. In this case, slow and steady is the fastest way to achieve sustainable, large-scale growth.

[ ] 1. Decide how much time you will be taking off within the next twelve months (minimum of four full weeks).

[ ] 2. Schedule this time off in your calendar.

[ ] 3. Make sure you actually take this time off. Don't defer, postpone or cancel these very important times.

[ ] 4. Identify your Foundation items.

[ ] 5. For each Foundation item above, build your Plan B contingency arrangement, in case something goes wrong with your current set-up. Do this for all of the Foundation items you have identified and for any others that come to mind.

[ ] 6. Identify which activities give you personal space.

[ ] 7. Plan and add your personal space activities into your weekly schedule. Treat these times as just as important as any other business appointments you normally conduct.

[ ] 8. Start building or adding to your personal financial reserves.

[ ] 9. Take steps to pay down debt—and set aside savings at the same time.

[ ] 10. If you don't already have one, get a personal financial advisor to help you build a financial plan.

[ ] 11. Build a list of potential sources of capital, including possible amounts, time frames and financial terms. Keep this list current at all times.

[ ] 12. Use *The Capacity Protector*™ to free up your mental energy.

[ ] 13. Track your activities for one week using the Activity Inventory Template.

[ ] 14. Rank your activities using the Activity Ranking Template.

[ ] 15. Identify the activities that can be delegated, and to whom they can be delegated.

[ ] 16. If needed, hire as necessary to free yourself up for higher-leverage roles within your company.

[ ] 17. If hiring someone new, make sure you find a person with skills complementary to yours, rather than someone with similar skills (and deficiencies).

[ ] 18. Complete the various questionnaires in the book.

[ ] 19. Calculate your goals for financial independence and financial significance.

[ ] 20. Collect financial information on your business.

[ ] 21. Identify the information that may not be currently tracked (gross profit per customer, for instance).

[ ] 22. Take steps to incorporate increased financial measuring and tracking in the future, changing your data collection systems as needed.

[ ] 23. Organize your financial statements into Excel spreadsheets consistent with the instructions in chapter 6.

[ ] 24. Analyze the financial statements to answer the questions in chapter 6.

[ ] 25. Organize and sort your customer data by quintiles in the two ways listed in chapter 6.

[ ] 26. Build your Credo.

[ ] 27. Clarify your Process and label it.

[ ] 28. Complete the exercise to clarify your desired customer experience of value.

[ ] 29. Conduct a customer satisfaction survey to clarify your actual customer experience of value.

[ ] 30. Develop your full package of marketing materials, including your:
[ ] Credo [ ] Process [ ] Credentials [ ] Testimonials
[ ] Other Pertinent Materials

[ ] 31. Draw your organization charts—one with names and one without.

[ ] 32. Answer the questions in chapter 8 in order to clarify the nature, scope and size of the organization you want to build.

[ ] 33. Draw an organization chart for the largest size of business you can conceive (roles only).

[ ] 34. Build your Income Statement and Balance Sheet for the company at this largest size.

[ ] 35. Draw the organization chart for your company at half your largest intended size.

[ ] 36. Build your Income Statement and Balance Sheet for this latest size of company.

[ ] 37. Build an organization chart (if not already done) for the company at two times your current size.

[ ] 38. Build the Income Statement and Balance Sheet for the company at twice your current size.

[ ] 39. Match up the current organization chart (with names) to the one for two times your current size.

[ ] 40. Clarify who might move where and the growth and development in your people that will be needed as you grow.

[ ] 41. Clarify your priorities for hiring new staff, making these decisions event-specific.

[ ] 42. Build a cash flow forecast for the next twelve months of your business.

[ ] 43. Determine any increased borrowing needs and handle these well in advance of when you may need the funds.

[ ] 44. Monitor your progress month by month along the way, as you implement your growth strategies.

[ ] 45. Enjoy your new-found profit and increased freedom!

No matter how overwhelming (or exciting) this may seem, by taking things once step at a time, you will keep moving and more-effectively achieve your goals.

Now, get started, and enjoy!

Kaizen CONSULTING

Are you ready to take your business to the next level?

For over 15 years, Kaizen Consulting has helped hundreds of entrepreneurial business owners to take their businesses to the next level. If you would like to explore the possibilities, please contact us:

Tel: (604) 263-5670
Email: info@kaizenconsulting.com

www.KaizenConsulting.com

Notes:

Manufactured by Amazon.ca
Acheson, AB